JESUS

Share Him with a Friend
Student Journal

CONTENTS

W9-CVX-935

Accelerated Spiritual Growth for Individuals and Families

Written by Randy Petersen, Jim Hancock and Mitch Vander Vorst

Editor: Mitch Vander Vorst
Cover Illustration: Thomason Design Center
Cover Design: De Leon Design
Text Design: PJK Design

Copyright © 2000 by Mainstay Church Resources
Published by Mainstay Church Resources

All rights reserved. No portion of this book may be reproduced in any form or by any means—electronic or mechanical, including photocopying, recording, or information storage and retrieval systems—without written permission of Mainstay Church Resources, Box 30, Wheaton, IL 60189-0030, (630) 668-7292.

Unless otherwise indicated, all Scripture quotations are taken from the *Holy Bible*, New Living Translation, copyright © 1996. Used by permission of Tyndale House Publishers, Inc., Wheaton, Illinois 60189. All rights reserved.

Scripture quotations marked (NIV) are taken from the HOLY BIBLE, NEW INTERNATIONAL VERSION®. NIV®. Copyright © 1973, 1978, 1984 by International Bible Society. Used by permission of Zondervan Publishing House. All rights reserved.

The goal of Mainstay Church Resources is to facilitate revival among God's people by helping them develop healthy spiritual habits in nine vital areas that always characterize genuine times of spiritual awakening. To support this goal, Mainstay Church Resources provides practical tools and resources including the annual 50-Day Spiritual Adventure, the Seasonal Advent Celebration, and the Pastor's Toolkit.

Printed in the United States of America

www.helpingpastors.com
ISBN 1-57849-174-6

Image is nothing.
Thirst is everything.
Obey your thirst.®

That's brilliant. The people who sell Sprite® know that we're sick and tired of all the hype. We're too smart to believe that some sneakers will put us in pro hoops, that a particular breath mint will dazzle our friends, or that a soft drink will let us live "on the edge." *Image is nothing.* And so this company creates an image that's anti-image. Very clever.

We can learn something here as we try to get our friends interested in Jesus.

First, we need to recognize that people may already have an image of Christianity, and not a good one. They may think of Christians as angry, antiquated androids, or as boring, bigoted bullies, or as crazy, clueless complainers. We could go on, but I'm sure you don't want to get all the way to zealous, zit-faced zeroes.

Our instinct, then, is to change our image. Let's show how cool Christians can be. And so we dress like the cool people, rap like the cool people, and try a little too hard. We end up presenting the Gospel of Coolness, but sometimes Jesus gets left out.

Image is nothing. So ditch coolness. Don't be something you're not. Instead, be the person you *are*, the person Jesus has made you. Share Jesus as he really is. No additives. No preservatives. Just 100% pure Jesus!

Thirst is everything. People are thirsty for Jesus. Maybe not everyone, and some may not know it's Jesus they're thirsty for, but you walk past some kids every day who want to hold on to something real, something powerful, something that will mean something. Maybe they're looking for it in a bottle or a gun or a needle or the back seat of a car. Maybe they're trying to earn it with good grades or school activities or nonstop parties. Whatever. They're really thirsty for Jesus.

Christians are like mirrors. People should be able to see Jesus' reflection in us. The problem with antiquated, bullying, complaining Christians is that the image gets muddied and people can't see Jesus through all that junk. The same can be true when we try to be "cool Christians." The mirror may be decorated with pretty designs, but it's still hard to see Jesus in it. What if we cleaned the mirror, so that people could see the real Jesus living in our lives? They might just fall in love with him.

That's what this 50-Day Spiritual Adventure is all about. Over the next seven weeks you'll be challenged to share the beautiful Jesus with others—not by creating some image to wow them, but simply by letting him live through you. Show people the real, refreshing Savior, and see if they *obey their thirst.*

How This Journal Can Change Your Life

This is more than an ordinary Bible study you're holding. It's a road map to accelerated spiritual growth—a Spiritual Adventure that can change your life. We trust that two months from now, you'll feel more closely connected to Jesus and be excited about new ways to introduce him to others.

After finishing the Adventure, you should have established at least one new healthy spiritual habit. If you can accomplish that in one strategic area of your spiritual life, you will have made enormous progress. And that's what this Adventure is all about: accelerating your spiritual growth, making spiritual progress, and developing your relationship with the Lord. So make it your goal to establish at least one new healthy spiritual habit. On page 5 you'll find suggestions for setting a specific goal.

What do I need to do? First, you'll need to read the suggested Bible verses each day and answer the questions in the journal. We also recommend that you choose some Bible verses to memorize. One per week is a good goal to shoot for. *The Jesus Student Scripture Pack* contains 22 verses for you to choose from (see p. 19).

Why are these action steps so powerful? The Adventure works well when you follow the five action steps, but you may choose to customize them to fit your situation. If one step is driving you crazy, forget it and focus on the others. Better to have four important life changes than five noble attempts cut short by a nervous breakdown! But if you can handle more, do it! (For a quick overview of all the Adventure assignments, see p. 7.)

How much time is involved? We estimate it takes just 10–15 minutes per day to complete the daily journal assignments. And you'll need a few additional time blocks during the 50-day period to complete some action steps. Does that sound like too much? We hope not. As with any important relationship, it's hard to grow closer to Christ if you don't devote priority time to him each day.

How do I keep track of everything? We will prompt you every day throughout this journal with a checkup to help you keep current with the action steps. Take the Adventure one day at a time, and you'll be fine.

Do I need to follow the journal every day? Yes. But if you miss a day or two, don't panic! It's best to pick up the journal entries with the current day, rather than try to make up those you've skipped.

Can I Adventure with my friends or family? Absolutely. That's a great way to make the study even more meaningful. It will take some extra time as you discuss the Bible verses or review one another's progress on the action steps, but the mutual accountability and encouragement will be a great benefit.

What can I do to keep going when the Adventure is over? Once you've finished the Adventure, you will undoubtedly want to continue with the spiritual habits you've developed over these 50 days. On the inside back cover we offer some great ideas to help you keep going. One suggestion is simply to repeat this Adventure by getting another journal to write in. That way you can cement what you've learned and turn those new spiritual habits into permanent, long-term benefits.

Where should I start? Familiarize yourself with the five action steps on pages 8–14. You might also flip through the day-to-day section of the journal beginning on page 20. Then give yourself a head start with the warm-up exercises on Friday and Saturday before Day 1 (pp. 15–16).

Using Spiritual Goals to Accelerate Your Growth

The Lord can use the next 50 days to help you establish at least one new healthy spiritual habit, if you let him teach you how. By applying the process of goal-setting to one strategic area of your spiritual life, you can make enormous progress toward a deeper, more intimate relationship with Jesus. Here's how. Prayerfully ask God which aspect of your spiritual life he wants to develop. Then follow these four simple steps.

1. Identify a specific goal.
2. Write it down in the space provided (below).
3. Determine a plan of action to help you reach your goal.
4. Have the resolve to stick with it.

These four steps help you use goal-setting to achieve accelerated spiritual growth.

What is the area of your spiritual life where you believe God most desires to see you mature? Is it prayer, daily Bible study, encouraging or serving others, sharing your faith? What specifically would you like to see happen? State this as your spiritual goal.

My goal for the 50-Day Spiritual Adventure is to:

Now consider how the Adventure can help you reach your goal. Review the Adventure Preview on the next page, or flip through the action step descriptions on pages 8–14. One or more of the assignments should provide you with an appropriate plan of action. If you don't find what you need there, create your own plan of attack.

My action plan:

Finally, resolve to follow through with your plan, asking the Holy Spirit to empower you. But don't get caught in the perfectionist trap. Studies show that it takes 21 days to establish a habit, good or bad. So this 50-Day Adventure allows you some grace time. Just pick up where you left off, and celebrate the progress you make with God's help.

How to Use This Journal

PRAY that God will help you show the real Jesus through your life. Ask him which of the eight themes *he'd* really like to see you pay special attention to during this Adventure.

COMMIT yourself to this Adventure. Take it seriously. If you give it some time and attention, you'll be rolling in the payoff. Check it out for a few days, and then try to get solid before the first week is over.

GET REAL. Be honest with yourself, and with God, as you answer the questions in this journal. Use codes if you're afraid of a snoop.

RELAX. If you miss a day, don't go crazy trying to make it up. Just get going on the current day. Later you can go back and see what you missed.

CONNECT with others. Try doing this Adventure with a few friends or your youth group. You can keep tabs on each other and pool new ideas and support.

PREPARE yourself by taking a look at the journal now, especially pages 8–14. During the Adventure, you'll take five action steps. Some may be fairly basic and familiar; others involve more prep. But don't worry! Every day the checkup in your journal will keep you on track.

The top of each daily page has a place for the date. Take a second to locate a calendar. Find the Sunday you plan to begin the Adventure. Write that date in the blank on Sunday, Day 1. Then write the dates, in order, on all the pages that follow.

EXPECT to grow. Great things can happen to you as you do this Adventure. God moves in powerful ways when people let him work through them. He can make a big difference in *your* life, too.

ASK questions. Don't expect to get all the info the first time through. There may be some things that you don't know, don't get, or want to remember to revisit. Write down these things in the margin of your journal or in your prayer file. But don't just write them down and forget about them. Try to revisit them or get them answered—do some research on your own, ask someone who might be able to help, or talk it through in your youth group or at church.

Adventure Preview

Over the next 50 days, this journal will focus on eight themes about Jesus and who he really was and is. And the five action steps will help you use *your* life to share Jesus with your friends.

THE THEMES

(How can we be attractive like Jesus? We can ...)
1. Reach Up (pp. 17–18)
2. Move Around (pp. 26–27)
3. Stand By (pp. 34–35)
4. Kneel Down (pp. 44–45)
5. Speak Out (pp. 52–53)
6. Look Ahead (pp. 60–61)
7. Follow Through (pp. 68–69)
8. Rise Above (p. 76)

THE ACTION STEPS

1. Open a Prayer File (p. 8)
2. Walk Around Walls (p. 10)
3. Brag on Someone (p.11)
4. Do Unto Others (p. 12)
5. Find the Story Behind the Story (pp. 13–14)

ADVENTURE ASSIGNMENTS

EVERY DAY

Read the assigned Bible passages and answer the questions in the journal.

Open a Prayer File and pray the Show Me Prayer (see pp. 8–9).

Brag on Someone by saying encouraging things that make people feel good (see p. 11).

EVERY WEEK

Walk Around Walls by doing a prayer walk around your school or neighborhood (see p.10).

Do Unto Others by sharing the love of Jesus in a practical way (see p. 12).

ONCE

Find the Story Behind the Story through discussing the deeper issues of a movie (see pp. 13–14).

BONUS

Memorize Bible verses that help you remember who the real Jesus is and how you can use your life to share him with a friend. Consider using the Jesus Student Scripture Pack to keep some important Bible verses with you throughout the day (see p. 19).

For a complete description of the action steps, see pages 8–14.

Open a Prayer File

Every Day

Where exactly is cyberspace? When you send an e-mail to a friend and they don't read it for a while, where does it sit? Is there really a kind of mailbox somewhere where the bytes of that message hang out until they're opened? You might be wondering the same sort of thing about prayer. Where do your prayers go? What difference do they make? When you pray, is there a heavenly computer that logs the prayer and zaps divine energy to the person you're praying for?

If e-mail seems mysterious, p-mail (prayer) is even more so. But the simple fact is, it works. The Bible doesn't give us all the inner workings of it; we're just told to bring our requests to God. It's not a magic wand, but it can make things happen. Often God surprises us in the way he chooses to answer our prayers.

More than anything, prayer is a *connection*. We log on with God for a while and start to think the way he thinks. It's a two-way thing. We send our messages, but we receive some too. Prayer makes a difference in our world, but it also changes *us*, and God helps *us* change the world. Sometimes we become the answers to our own prayers.

So don't treat prayer like a chore. Start tapping into its power. If you truly want to share Jesus with those around you, you'd better start connecting with him on a daily basis.

GET BUSY

Literally, open a "prayer file" on your computer. (Make it a word-processing document that you'll keep adding to.) Each day of this Adventure, pray in front of the computer. (Don't pray *to* the computer, just in front of it.) Ask God for guidance and listen for his response—in fact, type in what you think he's telling you.

If you don't have access to a computer, you can do the same basic things by writing in a notebook. Grab a cup of joe and curl up with this journal and a notebook or pad of paper for a good time with God. But high-tech or low, be sure to pray especially for any friends who still need to know Jesus.

The Show Me Prayer on the next page may help you start your prayer time each day, but make it your own and make sure to take some time to listen for answers.

Here are a few other things you might try as you pray in front of the computer.

Memos to Me. What God seems to be telling you as you pray.

2 Do. Is God giving you any assignments?

Flash Mail. Does someone come to mind during your prayer that may need a word of encouragement or challenge? If so, send him or her a quick note or e-mail.

Prayer Archive. Type in what you're praying for so you can check in later and see how God answered.

The Show Me Prayer

Lord, please show me how to live today.

Show me what you want me to learn.

Show me how you want me to see the world.

Show me the people you want me to touch with your love.

Show me how you want to work through me today.

In Jesus' name, Amen.

Walk Around Walls

Every Week

It's one of those survival camps and the Red Team is rushing through an obstacle course in the woods. They come to a big wall. "How will we ever get over this?" says the team leader, nicknamed G.I. Jane. But soon she has a plan. Using boulders and branches and a human pyramid, she finally grabs the top of the wall and hoists herself over. After jumping down the other side, Jane is surprised to see another teammate already there—the nonathletic Buster. "How did you get past the wall?" she asks.

"Easy," he answers. "I walked around it."

We face all sorts of obstacles in our lives, but sometimes we work way too hard. Who says we have to climb all the walls? The solution may be as simple as "walking around" it.

Let's talk about sharing Jesus with others. You've probably faced huge walls. People of other religions. People who think you're weird. People who couldn't care less. Now, you can badger and preach and argue all day long, but you're probably not going to scale these walls. Maybe you need a different approach.

When Joshua led the Israelites into the Promised Land, they ran up against the mighty walled city of Jericho. They didn't storm those walls; they walked around. And around. And around. Once a day, and seven times on the weekend. Circling that city, they marked it out for God, and the walls came a-tumblin' down.

Take the challenge of literally walking around your school or your neighborhood, inviting other believers to come along, praying as you go. You'll be amazed at the walls that will crumble.

GET BUSY

Once a week during the Adventure, do a prayer walk around your school or neighborhood, praying for the people there, especially those who need to know Jesus. You might think in terms of five houses on your block, apartments in your building, or a single building at school. Maybe later you can extend that, but start small and work your way up.

Just walk and talk to the Lord about the lives each place represents. If you know about needs, pray specifically. If you don't, pray generally. Ask God to break through any barriers keeping schoolmates and/or neighbors from good relationships with one another or with him.

You can do this alone, but it's better if you invite other Christians to join you. And make a point of inviting Christians from other churches, and other denominations. (That's another "wall" we can walk around.) Welcome anyone who wants to pray for your school or community.

This action step is part of a larger movement across North America. To find out more, here are two Web sites: www.lighthousemovement.com and www.challenge2000.org. If you have the opportunity, list Mainstay Church Resources as a ministry you'd like to affiliate with. That way you can stay in touch with the 50-Day Adventure.

Brag on Someone

Brag on Someone

Every Day

The guys were loners, people say. Losers. No one had a kind word to say to them. They buried their minds in fantasies of anger and violence. And then they grabbed some guns and bombs and shot up their high school.

Sad but true. That story has been played out, with minor variations, in too many schools, communities, and post offices throughout our land.

Flip the coin and consider a brighter side. Thousands of people in successful careers today—rocket scientists, ministers, musicians, accountants, teachers—will tell you they owe it all to some encouraging word they heard as kids. Someone dared to say, "Yeah, you're good at that," and so they applied themselves with greater confidence.

That's the effect Jesus had on people around him. He didn't scold people for being bad (except those who were scolding others); he encouraged people to change their lives and follow him. In the corrupt tax collector, in the guilty adulteress, even in his bickering buddies, he looked past the problems and saw the possibilities.

You know how good it feels when someone compliments you. It makes your day! So think about the power you have to compliment others. You have the power of joy at your disposal—use it! You might just turn a loser into a winner.

GET BUSY

"Brag on someone" every day of the Adventure. Compliment people. Say something encouraging that makes them feel good about themselves. On pages 40–41 you will find a Bragging Chart for you to keep a record of your bragging.

See if you can brag on a different person each day—that's 50 different people. And at least once a week, try to reach out of your normal environment—friends or clique—and compliment someone who is an outsider to you.

Surface comments may come easily: "You look nice today." But try to dig deeper for a meaningful comment about a person's attitude or effort: "You work so hard at this course; that's really an inspiration to me." Learn to look at people through Jesus' eyes. How would he brag on them?

Do Unto Others

Every Week

Jen and Erin were walking home from school as Jen spouted her latest complaints. "You know who cornered me in the cafeteria today? One of those *Super Christians*. I mean, he was wearing one of those WWJD shirts and everything."

Erin interrupted her: "You've got a lot of books to carry. Why don't I take some?"

Jen continued: "Christians think they're all that. Like they know and you don't."

They stopped at the store for their daily soda, but there was only one left. "You go ahead," said Erin.

Jen was now ranting about politics, and how Christians keep trying to impose their views on everyone else. Erin didn't say much, but when a skater zoomed past them, it was she who stepped aside to give him room, getting her shoes muddy so Jen wouldn't have to. When they reached her house, Jen suddenly exclaimed, "Oh, no! My mom took her laptop to work, which means I can't work on that report for history."

"Come on over to my place," offered Erin. "Use my computer. I'll do my work later."

And so they trooped over to Erin's house, where Jen was treated like royalty, offered snacks and drinks and access to the Internet. Of course she went on and on about her lunchtime encounter with that "obnoxious" Christian. But finally she stopped and asked, "Erin, I've noticed that you've been especially nice to me in the last week or so. You keep doing kind things. What's that about?"

"Well," Erin blushed, "funny you should mention that. I was afraid to tell you. You see, I'm a Christian. And about a week ago I decided to start living the way Jesus would want me to."

GET BUSY

Start by reading John 13:1–17—the story of Jesus washing his disciples' feet. Then follow his example by doing an act of service for someone each week. But just to make it interesting, we'll give you some guidelines. Be creative!

Week One (Days 1–6): Do an act of service that involves a towel. Maybe wash a neighbor's car or dry dishes or take your little sister to the beach.

Week Two (Days 7–13): We read about this in the thirteenth chapter of John. There's nothing unlucky about that. Do an act of service this week that involves the number 13. Send 13 e-mails of encouragement. Spend 13 minutes each day asking your parents about their day, and really listening to their answers. Find a person with size 13 shoes and shine them.

Week Three (Days 14–20): Jesus knelt to wash feet, so do an act of service that involves knees or feet. You could walk to the store for your grandmother, clean the crawl space on your hands and knees, or teach the kid down the block to play soccer.

Week Four (Days 21–27): Jesus used a basin to wash feet, so do an act of service that involves a basin or bowl of some kind. Give a teacher a bowl of fruit, take the special ed. class bowling, or clean your toilet.

Week Five (Days 28–34): Spend the first five days praying, asking God whom you should serve and how. Then follow his instructions.

Week Six (Days 35–41): Sometimes people jump into serving situations without thinking. As a result, people get "served" in ways they don't want. Take a few days to study people around you, looking for needs that you might meet. Then do an act of service that seems to be needed.

Week Seven (Days 42–50): In all of these acts of service, we're following the lead of Christ. Now it's time to let someone know that. Do an act of service and let the person know you're doing it because you're a Christian. You're just sharing the love of Jesus in this practical way.

Find the Story Behind the Story

Once

Remember *Titanic?* Big boat. Big boat sinks. Leonardo. Do you remember now? It was this big movie, right? Before *Phantom Menace?* Everyone was talking about it.

Well, there were some problems with *Titanic* the movie, but it was basically a story about salvation. This poor little rich girl didn't really have a life until Jack appeared. Ultimately, he died for her, and he changed her life forever. At the end, the elderly Rose says, "He saved me in every way a person can be saved."

It wasn't a "Christian movie." Far from it. But a savvy Christian could use this film to talk with friends about how *Jesus* "saved me in every way a person can be saved."

And, speaking of the new *Star Wars* flick, isn't that basically about good and evil? As a Christian, what "force" can "be with you"? *The Phantom Menace* isn't the full expression of spiritual truth, but it raises issues that you can talk about with your friends.

Many people go to movies and merely see the surface. Adventure. Witty lines. A hottie star. Explosions. But all movies tell stories, and you can use those stories to tell the "greatest story ever told"—the story of Jesus. Look for the story behind the story, and you'll be amazed how easy it will be to talk about the Greatest Action Star of Them All.

GET BUSY

Once during the Adventure, talk with non-Christian friends about a deeper meaning you see in a movie you've all seen. (You might substitute a video, TV show, or song.) This might happen naturally in a conversation at school, or you could plan a movie going or video night for a bunch of friends. There are some tips for you on the next page.

Tips for Movie Conversations

1 *Practice.* If you're uneasy with this whole idea, you may want to run through it a few times with *Christian* friends first. Make a list of movies you've seen or your favorite TV shows and talk about any spiritual issues that come up. Once you get the hang of it, it's not so hard.

2 *Get the brochure.* We've prepared a brochure to help you with this. It will guide you as you look for the story behind the story in the movies you see. Ask your youth leader or pastor about the brochure, or call Mainstay Church Resources at 1-800-224-2735.

3 *Listen first.* When you get into your movie discussion, don't jump in with all your ideas right away. Your friends may feel ambushed. Listen to the ideas they come up with. You may be surprised at the things they say all on their own.

4 *Don't preach.* If your friends feel you're trying to force your religion on them, they'll shut down the discussion. But as different people are sharing their opinions, you can certainly share yours. Use I-language. Say, "This reminded me of the story of Jesus . . ." or something like that, instead of "Here's what it means."

5 *Get past "thumbs-up or thumbs-down."* Everybody likes to rate the movies they see—Is it good? Is it "Christian"? How many bad words in it?—but try to steer the discussion beyond that. Talk about the decisions the characters make, the issues of right and wrong, the need for salvation of one kind or another, and so on.

6 *Be smart about offensive material.* Some movies are rough in the language they use or in their portrayal of sexuality or violence. Do your homework so you know in advance what to expect (and what offensive films to avoid). But if you do find yourself watching objectionable material with non-Christian friends, remember your purpose. Try to focus on aspects of the movie that could open up a spiritual discussion, and point the conversation toward Jesus.

Warm-up

Read Mark 3:7–12.

1 What do you think it was that made Jesus so attractive to people?

2 What qualities did Jesus have that would make him attractive to people today?

3 What kinds of people today are sought out by large, enthusiastic crowds?

4 What do you think the average person on the street thinks of Jesus today? What do they think about Christians?

5 If Jesus were ministering on earth today, do you think he would get the same kind of response he received in this account? Would you want to go see him? Why or why not?

6 Briefly skim the themes and action steps (see p. 7) you will be going through on this Adventure. Do any of these stand out for you? If so, which ones and why?

Checkup

____ I read introductory pages 1–14.
____ I read today's Bible passage.
____ I answered the questions in the journal.
____ I opened my prayer file and prayed the Show Me Prayer
(Action Step 1, pp. 8–9).

Read Matthew 4:1–11.

1 How did Jesus respond when tempted by the Devil?

2 Why do you think it is important to stay connected with God?

3 List one or more significant temptations you regularly face. How might your response to these temptations affect your connection to God?

4 What role does the Bible play in your efforts to overcome temptation? What steps could you take to make this resource more readily available?

5 Action Step 1 of this Adventure is to Open a Prayer File (see pp. 8–9). What struggles do you foresee in committing to a few moments of prayer each day for the next 50 days? What benefits do you think there will be?

6 You've just won the Adventure Games. You can make any Adventure wish and get it. What would your wish be for this Adventure?

Checkup

___ I read introductory pages 1–14.
___ I read today's Bible passage.
___ I answered the questions in the journal.
___ I opened my prayer file and prayed the Show Me Prayer (Action Step 1, pp. 8–9).

Theme 1:
Reach Up

Theme 1:
Reach Up

Let's write our own action thriller screenplay, okay? *Mission: Incredible* or something like that. Our hero, who looks something like Keanu Reeves, is on a train winding through the mountains of Europe, carrying munitions to a small group of freedom fighters in the Swiss Alps. Of course the train is rigged with a bomb, set to go off in ninety seconds, just enough time for the soundtrack to get really suspenseful.

Keanu (or whoever) knows nothing about bombs, so he whips out his cell phone and calls his old partner, who looks a lot like Sandra Bullock—kind of shy and mousy. And she's a bomb expert, too.

So, with modern technology beaming the signals off a satellite to a moving train half a world away, Sandra (or whoever) tells our hero to disconnect the red wire first—no, the blue one—as the seconds tick away. In a life-or-death situation, he trusts her to guide him properly, defusing the danger and making the world safe for Alpine skiers everywhere.

But then the train goes through a tunnel. The link to the satellite is lost. Keanu can't hear Sandra anymore and he cuts the wrong wire. Oops. Big explosion. Avalanche. Half of Europe destroyed. The end.

All right, so maybe we'll have to edit that script a bit. But it gives us a picture of the importance of uplinks. To get the right guidance, you have to stay connected—whether you're disarming bombs or sharing Jesus with your friends.

Reach up through prayer and Bible study to get your daily instructions from God. That's what Jesus did. Here and there throughout his busy ministry, we see him getting away to pray. And he always comes back with a new surge of purpose and direction. Tempted in the desert, he answers with the words of Scripture. Entertaining second thoughts the night before his crucifixion, he spends time with his Father and responds, "Your will be done."

He taught his disciples to do the same thing, asking for daily bread (which may imply asking on a daily basis), and praying, "Your kingdom come, Your will be done." We should be regularly connecting with God not only for our everyday needs, but also to set our agendas. Where does he want you to go today? How will you advance his kingdom, accomplish his will, "on earth as it is in heaven"?

Any effort to share Jesus with your friends, classmates, or neighbors is doomed unless you're getting your guidance from above. If you forget that God is leading you, it's like cutting the wrong wire; it'll blow up in your face. Some Christians are very good at announcing the one right way to evangelize. The problem is that God may have a different plan for you. Sharing Jesus with your friends may be something very subtle or maybe not. The point is that only God knows that. So give him a listen. Check in daily with him—*hourly*, if you can—to get the guidance you need.

FAQ: How do you open a prayer file?

Jason tore into his new Adventure journal the first chance he got. The last Adventure kicked his faith to a new level. He was eager to see what this new one would mean.

The cover was simple enough: Jesus. What more could you want? But "Share him with a friend"—that made it sound like a breath mint or something. Jason knew it was tough to "share Jesus." Whenever he tried to talk about his faith, he got all tongue-tied. He felt a pressure to do this, but he also wanted to avoid being labeled "Bible Boy" by his mocking classmates. Jason had seen plenty of weird witnessing by other Christians—noisy preaching at people who didn't want to listen—and he didn't want to be like that. There had to be a better way.

Hmmm, he thought as he looked over the Action Steps: *Open a Prayer File, Walk Around Walls, Brag on Someone. I can do that. But it doesn't sound like witnessing.* He flipped through the booklet, glancing at the themes: *Reach Up, Move Around, Stand By, Kneel Down.* Cute. And then there were those lame stories again, called FAQs this time. Obviously the writers were trying to guess what questions the readers would have about the Adventure, but Jason doubted that they could understand the problem he was having. He knew he should share Jesus with his friends, but the thought of actually doing it scared him to death.

Day 1 he started with the prayer file, doing the whole computer thing. It was strange at first, sitting in the place where he wrote papers and played *Grand Turismo*, but *praying* this time. He named a file "Jpray" and he prayed the Show Me Prayer. Then he started typing in the names of people he prayed for. His family. His best friend. His youth leader and pastor. The refugees of the world. Then he stopped. Oh, yeah, he had a big crush on Lindsey, so sometimes he prayed for her, too. Who else?

Trish.

Where did that come from? Trish was a girl at school that no one liked because she behaved really weird. In history class she kept saying things that were way off the subject. Fashion-wise, she got stuck somewhere between Goth and geek—everything black except for white kneesocks. People made fun of her.

Pray for Trish.

Jason had never really talked to Trish, never paid much attention except to roll his eyes. Why would he have an impulse to pray for her?

He began thinking of Jesus reaching out to the poor and needy, the social outcasts. He loved the little slimeball Zacchaeus and the sick woman who touched his cloak. Would Jesus worry about weirdness or fashion sense?

"Reach out to Trish," Jason prayed. "I don't know what she needs, or what you can do for her, but just, like, be with her. Tell her you love her."

With that, he typed in T-R-I-S-H and saved the file.

Checkup

Check the line if you have completed the assignment.

_____ I read introductory pages 1–14.

_____ I did the warm-up days on pages 15–16.

_____ I read page 17–18 (Reach Up).

Daily Assignments:

Read the assigned Scripture passages and answer the questions in the journal.

Open a Prayer File and pray the Show Me Prayer (pp. 8–9).

Brag on Someone by saying something encouraging that makes them feel good (p. 11).

Assignments for This Week:

Walk Around Walls by doing a prayer walk around your school or neighborhood (p. 10).

Do Unto Others by sharing the love of Jesus in a practical way (p. 12).

Bonus: Memorize Bible verses that remind you of who Jesus really is and how you can use your life to share him with a friend. (Consider using The Jesus Student Scripture Pack to help you with this—see below.)

Before the End:

Find the Story Behind the Story through discussing the deeper issues of a movie (pp. 13–14).

POCKET THE PACK

The Jesus Student Scripture Pack

This handy pack is a great reminder of who Jesus was and is. You can carry 22 Adventure Bible verses and the Show Me Prayer with you wherever you go. And the pack is a great tool to help you memorize some of God's Word—then you will really be able to share Jesus with your friends.

Ask for this resource at your church, or call Mainstay Church Resources at 1-800-224-2735.

Read Mark 1:29–39.

1 From these verses, and from your imagination, fill in some entries on Jesus' "To Do" list.

2Do 2Day

Heal blind people
Explain to Peter about the sower and seeds

_____

_____

2 Why do you think it was important for Jesus to take time out from helping people to reach up to his Father?

3 How often in an average week do you take the opportunity to quietly spend time with God? What kinds of busyness get in the way?

4 If you haven't already spent some time today opening your prayer file (Action Step 1, p. 6), go ahead and do so now.

5 Action Step 1 asks you to spend some time each day "reaching up" and praying. How many minutes of each day do you think you can commit to doing this? Would it be easier for you to commit to do this at a specific time of the day? If so, when?

6 In what ways would your life be better if you followed through on spending more time with God?

Checkup

_____ I read introductory pages 1–14.
_____ I did the warm-up days on pages 15–16.
_____ I read pages 17–18 (Reach Up).
_____ I opened my prayer file and prayed the Show Me Prayer (pp. 8–9).
_____ I bragged on someone and recorded it on pages 40–41 (p. 11).
_____ I walked around walls this week (p. 10).
_____ I did unto others this week (p. 12).
_____ I memorized a Bible verse this week.

Day 2 mondaydate

Read Luke 6:12–16.

1 Jesus prayed all night! What kinds of things do you think Jesus could have been praying about that would take all night?

2 Have you ever stayed up most of the night talking with a friend? If so, what did you talk about?

3 If you were to commit a whole night to reaching up to God, what would you talk about?

4 List two people you know who aren't Christians that you can pray for during this Adventure. Remember to include them in your prayer file for Action Step 1 (pp. 8–9).

5 According to Luke 6:12–16 Christ spent the whole night in prayer before making his decision. What role has prayer played so far in your decision-making process?

Checkup
_____ I opened my prayer file and prayed the Show Me Prayer (pp. 8–9).
_____ I bragged on someone and recorded it on pages 40–41 (p. 11).
_____ I walked around walls this week (p. 10).
_____ I did unto others this week (p. 12).
_____ I memorized a Bible verse this week.

21

Day 3 tuesday date

Read Luke 11:1–13.

1 What strikes you in reading this Bible passage?

2 The Lord's Prayer as written here can be recited in fewer than 15 seconds, yet it includes several kinds of prayer. What are some of them (i.e., praise, etc.)?

3 Which elements of the Lord's Prayer do you most often use? How could your prayer life have the kind of balance reflected in the Lord's Prayer?

4 Take some time now to carefully read and reread each line of the Lord's Prayer in verses 2–4. How would you explain these verses to a 4-year old?

5 Reread verses 5–10. List the top three things you would like to put on your personal prayer list to ask God for during this Adventure. (Remember to include this in your prayer file for Action Step 1, pp. 8–9).

    1.

    2.

    3.

6 Take some time now to quietly pray the Lord's Prayer in verses 2–4.

Checkup

_____ I opened my prayer file and prayed the Show Me Prayer (pp. 8–9).

_____ I bragged on someone and recorded it on pages 40–41 (p. 11).

_____ I walked around walls this week (p. 10).

_____ I did unto others this week (p. 12).

_____ I memorized a Bible verse this week.

Day 4
wednesday date

Read John 12:44–50.

1 On the following chart, indicate how positively the kids at your school feel about Jesus, Christians in the school, and churches in the area.

Positive

Neutral

Negative
  Jesus   Christians   Churches

2 Jesus says, "I have come to save the world, and not to judge it." Do you think this is different from the way most people view Jesus? Explain.

3 Do you think most people think Christians are trying to save the world or to judge it? Why do you think that is so?

4 How can you become more sensitive to God's will? What effect might that have on the words you speak to others?

5 What distractions in your life make it difficult for you to be directed by God, as Jesus was?

6 On Day 2 of this Adventure you listed two people you know who aren't Christians that you can pray for during this Adventure. Why not do a simple act of service for one of these two for Action Step 4 this week (see p. 12).

Checkup

___ I opened my prayer file and prayed the Show Me Prayer (pp. 8–9).
___ I bragged on someone and recorded it on pages 40–41 (p. 11).
___ I walked around walls this week (p. 10).
___ I did unto others this week (p. 12).
___ I memorized a Bible verse this week.

Day 5 thursday date

Read John 17:1–26.

1 Name a time when you and others you cared about were heading into a period of difficulty. Did your relationships grow closer or more distant?

2 In this passage Jesus is about to be arrested and crucified. What verses show that this situation drew him even closer to God and to his disciples?

3 Which phrases in this prayer help you better understand how well Jesus reached up to the Father?

4 How did Jesus want his followers to reach up?

5 Who does Jesus pray for in verses 20–26? If Jesus' prayer is answered in your life, how will that affect the world around you?

6 Has there been a time when you have felt that you did not belong to the world and that the world hated you because you were a Christian? Explain. How could you find support from other believers?

Checkup

_____ I opened my prayer file and prayed the Show Me Prayer (pp. 8–9).
_____ I bragged on someone and recorded it on pages 40–41 (p. 11).
_____ I walked around walls this week (p. 10).
_____ I did unto others this week (p. 12).
_____ I memorized a Bible verse this week.

Day 6 friday date_____

Read John 5:16–23.

1 Why, in your own words, were the Jewish leaders so upset with Jesus (verse 18)?

2 What did Jesus mean when he said that the Son could do nothing by himself?

3 On a scale of one to seven, how connected do you usually feel with God? How connected have you felt this past week?

1 2 3 4 5 6 7   1 2 3 4 5 6 7
usually feel   felt this past week

4 Has keeping a prayer file helped you feel more connected to God? Explain.

5 Action Step 3 (see p. 11) of this Adventure is to brag on someone each day. How is that going for you? Who have you bragged on this week?

6 Today ends the first week of the Adventure. But this emphasis on reaching up to God will continue weekly as you complete Action Step 1. If you haven't yet "opened a prayer file," reread the directions on pages 8–9. When will you do this?

Checkup
_____ I did Days 1–6.
_____ I opened my prayer file and prayed the Show Me Prayer (pp. 8–9).
_____ I bragged on someone and recorded it on pages 40–41 (p. 11).
_____ I walked around walls this week (p. 10).
_____ I did unto others this week (p. 12).
_____ I memorized a Bible verse this week.
_____ I found the story behind the story (pp. 13–14).

Theme 2:
Move Around

When I (Randy) was in seventh grade, I walked each day to the big suburban junior-senior high school. My path cut through some back yards and alleys, and I had to step across a plank that bridged a small stream before climbing a ravine and reaching the school's athletic fields. Sometime that year my trip was stalled by a couple of smart-aleck high-schoolers who stood guard at the stream. I had to pay them a "toll" of 25 cents to walk across the plank.

This was just wrong, and I was incensed, but they were twice my size. They could easily throw me into the stream if they wanted. But I wouldn't pay the quarter. I left the stream and skirted the area, taking the long way to school.

About twenty years later I talked with a young man who had a similar, but much more serious, problem. Tito lived in a gang-infested area of Chicago, and there were certain streets he couldn't walk on without losing his jacket, his sneakers, or maybe his life.

It's wrong when groups of people claim common ground as their "turf," making it difficult for others to enter. We see this at the root of many recent conflicts in the world—Kosovo, Bosnia, Rwanda, Northern Ireland, South Africa. It's "us" against "them." People easily choose up sides and start to fight.

You may be seeing the same thing in your school or community, with different groups picking sides—blacks and whites, or rich and poor, or jocks and goths (or whatever the cliques in your school). In a situation like that, it's tough to move across the social boundaries to share the joy of Jesus. But that's exactly what Jesus did. He strode right past social and racial barriers to touch Samaritans, Gentiles, lepers, prostitutes—anyone who needed him.

Unfortunately, we Christians can create divisions even among ourselves. Each denomination claims its turf. To be a "real" Christian, we say, you have to do things our way. You have to become like us. You have to come to our church. You have to pay our toll to cross the bridge.

There are two big problems with this. First, it can keep people from coming to Jesus. If Baptists are badmouthing Methodists, people are likely to ignore both. Second, it keeps us from teaming up with one another. If we're all serving Jesus, even in our different denominations, why not work together?

Once Jesus' disciples tried to stop some guy who was driving out demons in Jesus' name. Why? "Because he was not one of us," they explained. But Jesus put an end to their cliquish thinking: "Anyone who is not against us is for us" (Mark 9:38–41).

There are enough walls standing between Jesus and the people who need him. Let's move around the walls that are already there instead of building even more walls with our disagreements. Let's join hands and join forces in offering our Lord's wall-bashing love to our world.

FAQ: What kind of walls do we need to walk around?

Ashley had started talking about this prayer walk a week earlier. "Sure, yeah, we're there," said her friends Lindsey and Kim. The three girls were the most serious kids in the youth group, always planning social outings or ministry projects. They made a good team: Kim had a winning personality, Lindsey was Miss Popularity, and Ashley was the brains of the operation, making sure all the details worked out.

"Wednesday, after school, we're walking," Ashley reminded her cohorts in church on Sunday. "Wear your walking shoes."

"Oh, I forgot to tell you," said Kim. "They called a yearbook meeting for Wednesday. Lindsey and I have to go." Lindsey nodded and giggled.

Ashley knew very well that they didn't *have* to go, but they both had their eye on Brad Tomkins, the yearbook editor. She was upset at their shallowness. "Don't you care about praying for the school?"

"We can pray other times," Lindsey said. "Why don't we reschedule the walk?"

"Wednesday's the only day," Ashley snapped. "We talked about this last week."

Kim put a calming hand on her shoulder. "You can go on without us. We're not the only ones in the youth group."

But Ashley was already counting the people who would decide not to walk because Kim and Lindsey weren't walking. There would probably be only two or three left, and those were people Ashley didn't really want to be seen with— much less doing something as crazy as walking around the school in prayer.

During lunch on Monday, Jason swung by Ashley's table. "We having the prayer walk on Wednesday?" he asked.

"Yeah, but Lindsey's not coming."

"Oh." Jason's disappointment was easily read.

"Are you still going?" Ashley asked. "You don't have to."

He made a decision at that moment. "Yes, this is important."

Shannon was sitting across the table. "What's this about a prayer walk?" she asked.

"We're getting some kids from our church to walk around the school praying," Ashley replied, sounding as if she was apologizing.

"Cool," said Shannon. "Could I come? Or is it just your church?"

This was a whole new idea for Ashley. Could it be that there were other Christians in the school, from other churches? "We'll be praying that people in the school would, like, come to know Jesus," she explained. "Like, become Christians."

"Yeah," said Shannon, with a big smile. "We pray for that in our church too. Could I bring some kids from my youth group?"

Ashley, the planner, suddenly had a whole new dimension to think about. Other Christians. Other churches. It was Jason who answered: "Yes, the more the merrier. We'll meet at the flagpole after school and then we'll just walk, like, around the tennis courts and behind the ball field, and we'll just, you know, pray."

Just then a guy named Keith sat down at the table with a tray full of cafeteria food. "What's this about praying?" he asked.

As Jason answered, Ashley was mapping out whole new worlds in her mind.

MOVE AROUND

Read John 4:1–42.

1 What good resulted from Jesus' conversation with the woman (verses 39–42)?

2 What walls did Jesus move around in this passage? (Check all that apply.)
_ Ethnic walls
_ Brick walls
_ Gender walls
_ Religious walls
_ Cultural walls
_ Climbing walls
_ Other _____

3 What was the result of Jesus' willingness to move around the walls in this passage?

4 What walls in your world don't you walk around very often? What walls do you walk around?

5 Action Step 1 for this Adventure is to open a prayer file (see pp. 8–9). Consider praying for God to show you one specific wall to walk around during this Adventure. Make sure to write down any answer you hear.

6 In verse 21 Jesus avoided feeding the flames of division and instead emphasized what was important (worshiping the Father in spirit and in truth). Do you think there are controversies and divisions between churches or Christians in which it would be best to "move around" and emphasize our common relationship with God? If so, name them.

Checkup
_ I read pages 26–27.
_ I opened my prayer file and prayed the Show Me Prayer (pp. 8–9).
_ I bragged on someone and recorded it on pages 40–41.
_ I walked around walls this week (p. 10).
_ I did unto others this week (p. 12).
_ I memorized a Bible verse this week.

Day 9
monday date

Read Luke 7:1–10.

1 This military commander was probably a Roman and definitely a Gentile. In Jesus' time, it was a disgrace for a Jewish rabbi to be approached directly by a Gentile. What did Jesus see in this man that was more important than anything else?

2 Action Step 2 for this Adventure is to walk around walls by doing a prayer walk each week (see p. 10). Who are some people you could consider inviting to do this with you this week?

_ Mother and/or father
_ Grandparents
_ Boyfriend/girlfriend
_ Al Gore
_ Best friend
_ Other friends

_ Your youth group
_ Other Christians at school
_ Brothers and/or sisters
_ Anakin Skywalker
_ Other_____

3 What plans have you made (or do you need to make) for your walk this week?

4 In what areas do you tend to rely on stereotypes or prejudge people?

_ The color of their skin
_ Their religion
_ The people they hang with
_ The clothes they wear
_ The cars they drive
_ Where they live
_ By their faith
_ What people say about them

_ What flavor of ice cream they like
_ The music they listen to
_ Gender
_ Intelligence
_ Athletic ability
_ Complexion
_ Their brand of toothpaste

5 Often we fail to see the potential in others because of stereotypes that cause us to dismiss them. What causes you to dismiss people prematurely?

6 How do you think you should look at people instead?

Checkup

___I opened my prayer file and prayed the Show Me Prayer (pp. 8–9).
___I bragged on someone (p. 11).
___I walked around walls this week (p. 10).
___I did unto others this week (p. 12).
___I memorized a Bible verse this week.

MOVE AROUND

Read Matthew 15:21-28.

1 What is the initial reaction of Jesus and his disciples to the request of the Canaanite woman, a Gentile? Do you find that a little surprising? Why or why not?

2 What does this passage teach about the importance of extending God's love to unlikely candidates, even if we have other priorities? Who in your school or community might fit into this category?

3 Write in exactly 17 words your thoughts and feelings about this passage.

4 Are there people in your world who would be grateful even for crumbs of physical, emotional, or spiritual healing? Who?

5 Do you know someone who could use healing? If so, who? How could you pray for this person? Don't forget to add him or her to your prayer file.

6 This week walk around a wall as you do unto others for Action Step 4 (see p. 12). What wall could you walk around to show God's love to someone in a practical way? How do you plan to do that?

Checkup

___ I opened my prayer file and prayed the Show Me Prayer (pp. 8-9).
___ I bragged on someone (p. 11).
___ I walked around walls this week (p. 10).
___ I did unto others this week (p. 12).
___ I memorized a Bible verse this week.

Day 11
wednesday date

Read Mark 9:38–41.

1 What does "Anyone who is not against us is for us" mean to you? Give at least three examples.

2 Is the "Whoever is not against us is for us" statement an attitude reflected by your church or youth group toward other churches or segments of society? If not, what stands in the way? What about your own attitude?

3 Who is someone today who appears to be doing good in Jesus' name even though he or she is not from your faith tradition? How do you feel about that?

4 What kinds of kindness (like the "cup of water") have you been shown?
_ Sister lets you watch crucial episode of *Buffy the Vampire Slayer*
_ Friend spends an evening helping you understand calculus
_ Youth leader reschedules meeting so you can go to Sixpence concert
_ Mom serves your favorite broccoli casserole
_ Neighbor lets you use sloping driveway for inline skating stunts
_ Dad ignores the strange odor in the car after you borrowed it
_ Other _____
_ Other

5 Every day for Action Step 3 you have been bragging on someone (see p. 11). Today, brag on someone who is on the other side of a wall from you or who has given you an unexpected "cup of water." Write their name here.

6 What kinds of walls exist in your school, and on what side of each wall are you (inside or outside)?

Checkup
___ I opened my prayer file and prayed the Show Me Prayer (pp. 8–9).
___ I bragged on someone (p. 11).
___ I walked around walls this week (p. 10).
___ I did unto others this week (p. 12).
___ I memorized a Bible verse this week.

Day 12
Thursday date

Read Luke 18:9–14.

1 Which person in this story would have seen Jesus as attractive? Which one would have seen him as unattractive?

2 How would this parable have shattered the stereotypes of those who were confident of their own righteousness and looked down on others?

3 Looking back, when is a time you acted like the Pharisee? When have you acted like the tax collector? Explain.

4 How would this parable be told as a news report on ABC—or on MTV's *The Tom Green Show?*

5 Have you ever witnessed an event where the proud have been humbled and the humbled have been honored? If so, explain. If not, why do you think that is?

6 What does it mean to you to be humble? In what areas of your life are you humble? In what areas are you proud?

Checkup

_____ I opened my prayer file and prayed the Show Me Prayer (pp. 8–9).
_____ I bragged on someone (p. 11).
_____ I walked around walls this week (p. 10).
_____ I did unto others this week (p. 12).
_____ I memorized a Bible verse this week.

Day 13 friday date

Read Luke 10:25–37.

1 If this were a modern-day movie, what would you call it, and what walls would it be about?

2 What real-life person would you cast as The Good Samaritan and why?

3 What song would you use as the title song and why?

4 Write a radio ad for the movie and when you're done read it out loud and try to get it to fill 29 seconds.

5 Are there any walls you feel especially called to walk around after completing this week of the Adventure? If so, write them down here and in your prayer file. If not, ask God to show you a wall before this Adventure is over.

6 What personal stereotypes of "us" and "them" has Jesus revealed to you this week that you need to move around?

Checkup

____I did Days 7–13.
____I opened my prayer file and prayed the Show Me Prayer (pp. 8–9).
____I bragged on someone (p. 11).
____I walked around walls this week (p. 10).
____I did unto others this week (p. 12).
____I memorized a Bible verse this week.
____I found the story behind the story (pp. 13–14).

Theme 3:
Stand By
Theme Stand By

Erika felt her English teacher wasn't treating her fairly. She worked really hard on every assignment, but Mr. Z gave her low grades. In class discussions, the few times he'd call on her, he seemed critical of her opinion. It wasn't right. After talking with her best friend Chrissy, Erika decided to confront her teacher. It was one of the hardest things she ever did.

Chrissy went with Erika to Mr. Z's classroom after school, standing there as she presented her complaints. The teacher listened, somewhat surprised that she felt that way. He didn't think he was overly critical, but he would try extra hard to be fair in the future.

Back in the hallway, Erika took a deep breath and said, "Thanks."

"For what?" Chrissy asked. "I didn't do anything."

"For standing by me. I couldn't have done it without you."

Having a friend just being there, standing ready to help, was a big comfort to Erika. It's true for most of the people you pass in the halls each day. How many of them feel they're outsiders? How many are afraid to try something because they don't have any support? How many think of themselves as the scum of the earth because there's no one telling them how great they are?

If you've ever tried gymnastics, you know that certain routines require a "spotter." What does the spotter do? Stands by. But just knowing that a spotter is there to help, ready to break a fall if necessary—that gives a gymnast the confidence to make some amazing moves. Everyone needs that kind of support in order to develop their abilities—in the gym, or in life.

Jesus supported people like that, and he specialized in the outcasts of society. The religious folks were horrified that he befriended prostitutes and slimy tax collectors—they called him a "friend of sinners." He looked past the problems and saw the possibilities.

As you read the Gospels, you get the feeling that Jesus genuinely liked people. Oh, he criticized bad behavior here and there, but he seemed to challenge people to be the best they could be. He didn't turn a blind eye to sin, but he extended his Father's deep, deep love to the sinners he met. When a cheating wife was brought before him, he stood by her, accusing those who accused her. Then he challenged her to "go and sin no more" (John 8:1–11).

Let's be honest. A lot of Christians nowadays don't seem to like people very much. We can be quick to point out sinful behavior when we see it, but we're often slow to offer support to sinners. Some say, "Love the sinner and hate the sin," but we seldom do that. We "hate the sin, and try to make the sinner feel as guilty as possible." How will people ever come to Christ if the Christ-followers keep treating them as guilty, sinning outsiders?

It's time to start showing people the radical love of Jesus. We need to see the possibilities in people and "stand by" them, complimenting them and supporting them, showering them with the kindness of our loving Lord.

FAQ: Can you compliment people you hardly know?

The prayer walk had turned out well. Jason was one of only five people from his own church who showed up. But word got around, and 25 other kids came, representing three or four different churches. There were Baptists and Methodists and Pentecostals, blacks, whites, Latinos and Asians. *A little snapshot of what heaven will be like*, Jason thought. They just walked and prayed and sang a few choruses that everyone seemed to know. It was a fabulous event, and everyone agreed they should do it next week.

By comparison, though, the third Action Step seemed like a piece of cake. Bragging on people is pretty easy to do, especially if you're a friendly kind of guy like Jason. No planning, no publicity, just be nice.

The first week or two, Jason complimented the people closest to him. "You draw really well," he told his pain-in-the-neck sister Nikki, who was twelve going on twenty-nine. She looked up from her latest artwork with a puzzled look. Why would her cruel big brother be nice to her? Then it dawned on her. "Oh, it's for the Adventure, right?"

"No, Nik," Jason protested, "I really mean it. But . . . yeah."

"Thanks anyway."

He told his mom how much he appreciated all her hard work as a single parent, and she gave him a big hug. He thanked his youth leader for teaching him the Bible in a fun way. He praised his best friend's sense of humor. He wrote a letter to his grandmother, called his favorite cousin, and even affirmed his history teacher after an especially interesting class.

Then he was stumped. Jason was trying to brag on 50 different people during the Adventure, and he had only reached 15. He decided to wing it for a couple of days, just waiting for opportunities to come up. And they did. One day a classmate did a great job on an English class presentation. The next day Lindsey looked especially lovely. The next day there were no good opportunities at school, but on the way home he stopped for a burrito and the girl at the counter was very cheerful, so he complimented her.

That night he sat at the computer, going through his prayer file.

"Lord, be with Mom and Nikki and Chris and Dave and Lindsey and, well, Trish—"
Say something nice to her. There was that feeling again, not a voice exactly, but he knew it was God talking to him. "Who, Trish?" he responded. *She needs a compliment.* "I hardly know her!" *And you're best buds with the burrito girl?* "No, but—I can't! She'll think I like her. Others will think I like her." *I like her.* "That's not what I mean!"

But the feeling would not leave him. The next day Jason sat in history class, glancing over at the weird girl in the corner. What could he possibly say to Trish? With five minutes left in the period, she joined the class discussion . . . in her own odd way. She compared the divisions in the U. S. before the Civil War with the divisions between groups of people today. As always, Trish wasn't explaining herself well, and everyone just stared at the ceiling as she spoke. Even the teacher just said, "Thank you. . . . anyone else?" But Jason got it! He knew exactly what she was saying, and it made a lot of sense.

He rushed over to talk with her after class. "Trish! What you said, it was really good. It was kind of, well, brilliant . . . maybe. I mean, I liked it. Thanks for, uh, saying that."

The look on the girl's face was priceless, as if someone had turned on a light in a long-dark room. "Yeah, you know, sometimes I think things but I'm not sure of what they mean, but I try to say it if it's good but it's not always what I expect, you know? So I'm never really sure and I never know what people are thinking, so wow, thank you a lot. Because sometimes I think . . ."

Jason was already backing away. "I've, uh, got to get to class." She was still talking.

Read Matthew 9:9–13.

1 Tax collectors would have been among the most reviled people in the culture during Jesus' time because they collected money on behalf of an occupying foreign government. They made a cushy living by collecting more tax than was required. Why did their behavior not prevent Jesus from associating with them?

2 The Pharisees asked the disciples why Jesus ate "with such scum." In your own words, what was Jesus' answer?

3 Let's dig a little. In verses 12–13, Jesus quotes an Old Testament verse. Look up Hosea 6:6 to see what it meant then. Why does Jesus use that verse here?

4 How good do you think your church or youth group is at welcoming "sick people" and "sinners" as well as "healthy people" and "those who think they are already good enough"? Explain.

5 Jesus stood by people who were outcasts and were not considered good enough. Is there someone or some group of people that Jesus has prompted you to stand by during this Adventure? If so, who, and what do you plan to do about it?

6 If you were one of the disciples and the Pharisees asked you "Why does your teacher eat with such scum?" how would you answer?

Checkup

___ I read pages 31–32.
___ I opened my prayer file and prayed the Show Me Prayer (pp. 8–9).
___ I bragged on someone (p. 11).
___ I walked around walls this week (p. 10).
___ I did unto others this week (p. 12).
___ I memorized a Bible verse this week.

Day 16
monday date

Read Mark 14:1–9.

1 How would you have expected Jesus to respond to the woman who poured perfume over his head? Why?

2 Jesus saw the beauty in the woman's actions while the disciples only saw an outsider wasting perfume. Now bring this into your world. Who or what group of people would the woman represent today? Who or what group of people would the disciples represent today?

3 Nowadays what extravagant gift might a teen give to Jesus?
  _ Entire collection of Jewel CDs
  _ New fully suspended mountain bike
  _ Courtside tickets to see Kobe Bryant and Shaq at the Staples Center
  _ A year of free coffee
  _ One year's salary
  _ A free piercing or tattoo at Lenny's Discount Body Shop (and a second one half off)
  _ Other _____

4 How easy on a scale of 1 to 5 (5 being really easy) is it for you to stand up for people when others are criticizing them or putting them down?

  1 2 3 4 5

5 Open your prayer file now and pray for one person you would like to stand up for more often. Write his or her name here also.

6 Is this person someone you could brag on for Action Step 3 (p. 11)? If so, what would you say, and how would you do it? If not, why?

7 Describe a time in your life when a disagreement with another Christian led to conflict. How might that situation have developed differently if all involved had looked for the best in one another?

Checkup
___ I opened my prayer file and prayed the Show Me Prayer (pp. 8–9).
___ I bragged on someone (p. 11).
___ I walked around walls this week (p. 10).
___ I did unto others this week (p. 12).
___ I memorized a Bible verse this week.

STAND BY

S T A N D B Y

Read Luke 19:1-10.

1 Describe a time when you felt unfairly judged by someone who failed to recognize your true potential.

2 What groups of people are treated like Zacchaeus today?
- _ IRS agents
- _ Politicians
- _ Gay people
- _ Teachers
- _ Deep-sea divers
- _ Parents
- _ Brothers and/or sisters
- _ Fast food cooks
- _ Geeks and/or nerds
- _ Jocks
- _ People with disabilities
- _ People over 23 years old
- _ Asian people
- _ TV news anchors
- _ Other

3 What groups of people are outsiders in your school? How about in your youth group or church?

4 Jesus showed in this passage that "standing by" is more than just eating lunch with an unpopular person in the cafeteria. It is believing in their potential. Think of someone you know in the "outcast" category and write about his or her potential.

5 Could you encourage this person by bragging on him or her today? (See Action Step 3, p. 11.) If so, you could just say, "I think you are really great ..." and fill in the potential you see.

6 Think of a non-Christian you know. Has your view of that person been more like the attitude of Jesus or more like the attitude of the people in verse 7?

Checkup
_____ I opened my prayer file and prayed the Show Me Prayer (pp. 8–9).
_____ I bragged on someone (p. 11).
_____ I walked around walls this week (p. 10).
_____ I did unto others this week (p. 12).
_____ I memorized a Bible verse this week.

Read Mark 5:1–20.

1 This demon-possessed man would have been a scary prospect for your average Christian to like and care for, but Jesus did just that. Why do you think Jesus took an interest in this man? Do you think he was scared? Explain.

2 What was the outcome of Jesus' care and compassion for the demon-possessed man?
  _ For the man:
  _ For Legion:
  _ For the pigs:
  _ For the herdsmen:
  _ For the community:
  _ For Jesus:

3 What kinds of people has our society given up on, leaving them to lives of physical, emotional, or spiritual pain?

4 Write more than 23 words about a time when you were an outsider and someone stood by you.

5 What's hard about standing by people who are different, or outsiders?

6 This man initially pushed Jesus away. There are many suffering people who push away those who are trying to help, but they desperately need someone who will stand by them. Is there someone like this that you know? What are ways that you could still be there for them, even if they push you away? (For example: leaving your phone number or e-mail address, sending them a note asking how they are, etc.)

Checkup

_____I opened my prayer file and prayed the Show Me Prayer (pp. 8–9).
_____I bragged on someone (p. 11).
_____I walked around walls this week (p. 10).
_____I did unto others this week (p. 12).
_____I memorized a Bible verse this week.

STAND BY ... STAND BY

Bragging Chart

Each day of the Adventure, record an encouraging or affirming remark you made to someone. For more information on Action Step 3, Brag on Someone, see page 11.

Sunday, Day 1
Monday, Day 2
Tuesday, Day 3
Wednesday, Day 4
Thursday, Day 5
Friday, Day 6

Saturday, Day 7
Sunday, Day 8
Monday, Day 9
Tuesday, Day 10
Wednesday, Day 11
Thursday, Day 12
Friday, Day 13

Saturday, Day 14
Sunday, Day 15
Monday, Day 16
Tuesday, Day 17
Wednesday, Day 18
Thursday, Day 19
Friday, Day 20

Saturday, Day 21
Sunday, Day 22
Monday, Day 23
Tuesday, Day 24
Wednesday, Day 25
Thursday, Day 26
Friday, Day 27

Bragging Chart cont'd

Bragging Chart cont'd

Saturday, Day 28

Sunday, Day 29

Monday, Day 30

Tuesday, Day 31

Wednesday, Day 32

Thursday, Day 33

Friday, Day 34

Saturday, Day 35

Sunday, Day 36

Monday, Day 37

Tuesday, Day 38

Wednesday, Day 39

Thursday, Day 40

Friday, Day 41

Saturday, Day 42

Sunday, Day 43

Monday, Day 44

Tuesday, Day 45

Wednesday, Day 46

Thursday, Day 47

Friday, Day 48

Saturday, Day 49

Sunday, Day 50

STANDBY

Read Mark 10:13–16.

1 What would the basic plot line be if this story served as the basis for an episode of *E.R.*, *Felicity*, *South Park*, or *Sesame Street* (pick one)?

2 Make a list of everyone you can think of that has stood by you.

3 Now, who can you say you've stood by in the last three months?

4 Who did you list in question 2 that you would like to brag on today or when the opportunity arises? What could you compliment or encourage him or her about? (Maybe you could just say, "Thanks for standing by me.")

5 What is one specific way you could be Christlike this week by affirming the potential of a child in your life?

6 Action Step 2 for this Adventure is to walk around walls by doing a prayer walk (see p. 10). If you haven't already done your walk this week, what plans have you made (or do you need to make)? What are you going to walk around?

Checkup

____I opened my prayer file and prayed the Show Me Prayer (pp. 8–9).
____I bragged on someone (p. 11).
____I walked around walls this week (p. 10).
____I did unto others this week (p. 12).
____I memorized a Bible verse this week.

Day 20

Read John 1:43–51.

1 How do you feel when someone makes a negative comment about your background? Why do you think Jesus could look past Nathanael's put-down of his hometown?

2 What was the first thing Philip did after Jesus called him to be a disciple?

3 How did Philip react to his friend's initial disbelief?

4 If you were going to pick twelve disciples for Jesus, what kind of people would you pick? (Check all that apply.)

_ Backstreet Boys
_ Fishermen
_ Prostitutes
_ Police officers
_ Tax collectors
_ Bikers
_ Lawyers
_ Movie stars
_ Denver Broncos
_ Accountants
_ Writers
_ Teachers

_ Mothers
_ CEOs
_ Artists
_ Social workers
_ Unemployed people
_ Factory workers
_ Doctors
_ Professional surfers
_ Construction workers
_ Other _____
_ Other _____

5 How did Jesus treat the people around him? What kind of people did he seem to stand by? (Go back and skim through the journal pages and Bible passages for this last week to help you answer.)

6 One of the reasons Jesus was attractive to so many is that he liked people and drew out the best in them. How have you mirrored his attitude and behavior this week?

Checkup

____ I did Days 14–20.
____ I opened my prayer file and prayed the Show Me Prayer (pp. 8–9).
____ I bragged on someone (p. 11).
____ I walked around walls this week (p. 10).
____ I did unto others this week (p. 12).
____ I memorized a Bible verse this week.
____ I found the story behind the story (pp. 13–14).

Theme 4:
Kneel Down
Theme Kneel Down

I (Randy) had it all planned out. I really wanted to tell my high school classmates about Jesus, but it was hard. They tuned me out. So I figured out a way to make them listen. I would become valedictorian and give a speech at graduation. Seriously! It must have been sophomore year when I decided this, and I already had a straight-A average. Keep it up two more years, and I could give a speech.

This must sound crazy to you, and it's embarrassing to me. It would have been a lot easier just to talk to the people in my classes, rather than trying to beat them out for top grades. As it turned out, I got my wish. Six of us had straight-A averages, so they let us all speak briefly. I used my two minutes to caution against reaching so far for success that you forget what's most important—your soul. "Reach for Jesus, and you're safe forever," I told my classmates.

Nowadays I'd get sued for that speech—then I was just ignored. I guess I expected people to be deeply touched by my mini-sermon. Maybe people would want to pray with me in the parking lot, giving their hearts to Jesus in response to my message. It didn't happen. Most of the kids just went out and got drunk.

But something else had been happening my senior year, though I didn't think much about it at the time. I had a friend named Skip. Well, his real name was Gene, but he was such a runt of a guy in junior high we nicknamed him Skippy, and it sort of stuck. Skip bore the brunt of our class's teasing for a couple of years. I wish I could say I stood up for him right away, but I was afraid to. Still, I was one of the first to befriend him.

Over the years he became more "normal" and we became better friends, and then all of a sudden, senior year, he became a Christian. Not really because of me, but maybe a little. And with his newfound Christian energy, we started a little Bible study group after school. No big revival or anything, but a few people were brought closer to Jesus.

Thanks for hanging with me for these reminiscences. There really is a point to all this. I had everything backwards. I thought I could testify for Jesus by being a star and making a speech. It didn't work. What worked was being a friend to some dork.

I've talked to lots of kids lately who want to become famous. As an acting teacher, I guess I deal with starstruck wannabe's. There's this feeling that they'll never do anything important until they're up there on some screen. *Then* people will pay attention to them. And some Christians get into that mindset: Become a famous actor/singer/athlete/politician and *then* people will hear what you have to say about Jesus.

Don't go that way. If you want to be a leader, Jesus said, be a servant. Look for the runt of your class, the kid everyone else is picking on, and serve that person. That will do more for Christ's kingdom than all the speeches you could ever give.

Ashley always tried to put forth an attractive image of Christianity, and it didn't hurt that her two best friends were among the most popular girls in the school. They knew kids in their youth group who carried big red Bibles and dressed 20 years behind the times. *If that's what a Christian looks like,* Ashley thought, *why would anyone want to become one?* They were trying to prove that people could stay true to their faith and still be cool. And they were definitely among the brightest and best in the school, involved in a full slate of activities.

Though she often stood in the shadow of her two friends, the school play gave Ashley a chance to shine. Starring as Marian the Librarian in *The Music Man*, she wowed the crowds. As might be expected, she let some of her Adventure work slip during the ultra-busy week of performance. She hadn't even thought about the "Do Unto Others" step when she went to the cast party Saturday night at the home of one of the chorus members.

But sometimes the best opportunities to serve happen by accident. On that night Ashley opened the wrong door. She was just looking for the bathroom; instead she stumbled into some sort of den where the tech crew was hanging out. In that school, techies generally stayed away from the actors. They were a whole different type of student—rowdier, less refined. While the cast was playing some 80s board game downstairs, upstairs the tech crew was playing spin the bottle—and "drink the bottle." That's right, they had smuggled in some alcohol. Ashley saw a couple of bottles there as she poked her head in.

"Sorry, I must be in the wrong place," she mumbled.

"Are you ever!" said a voice from the room.

"Hey, it's one of Charlie's Angels!" said someone else. That was their nickname for the three popular Christian girls. "No, you don't belong here." And anyone could see that—Ashley in her fashionable khaki party outfit and a dozen kids sprawling in black T-shirts and jeans, some shirts bearing the names of the hard-metal rock groups they worshiped.

"You know," she said, "you shouldn't be drinking." Like they cared what she said.

Ashley was about to head out the door, when she heard a faint voice: "I don't feel so good." Looking back, she saw a young girl lying on her side, her face turning colors that human skin was never meant to be. It was Ginny, a freshman who lived down the street from Ashley.

In the doorway, Ashley faced a moment of decision. She had gone through high school avoiding any contact with alcohol or drugs, and she was proud of her reputation as a devout Christian. Those kids were right, she didn't belong here. But what would Jesus do? The WWJD bracelet seemed to grab her wrist and lead her into the room, somehow to help, to serve.

Rushing in, she sat beside Ginny and started barking orders. "Somebody get me a wet cloth, a glass of water. She's burning up here. What was she drinking?" A few people who were sober enough to respond started moving. Ashley knelt beside Ginny to get a good look at her, and the girl threw up—all over Ashley's new clothes. Someone was offering a towel, and Ashley wiped Ginny's face, softly assuring her that everything would be all right.

One of the kids had run to get an adult from downstairs. When Mrs. Adams stepped into the room, she was surprised to see Ashley, the leading lady, kneeling there, covered with puke, smelling of liquor. She misunderstood at first, but then she saw the sick girl and began to help her.

In the following days, the drama department took disciplinary action against the kids who had brought the liquor to the party. Ginny got better, after her mild bout with alcohol poisoning. Ashley dropped by Ginny's house to see how she was, but stayed pretty quiet about the whole matter. Once, as she passed a couple of techies in the hall, she smiled and nodded as if they were friends—she had always ignored them before. She overheard the voices behind her:

"Who's that?"

"One of Charlie's Angels."

"No, that's Ginny's Angel."

KNEEL DOWN

Read John 13:1–17.

1 According to verses 12–17, what point was Jesus trying to get across by washing his disciples' feet?

2 What did Jesus mean when he said, "I have given you an example to follow. Do as I have done"?

3 What do you think would be the result if you followed the example of Britney Spears, Austin Powers, or Dennis Rodman (pick one)?

4 What in your world would you compare to the custom of washing feet? Why?

5 Has there been a time in your life when someone you felt was above or more important than you kneeled down to serve you? If so, what was that experience like?

6 Sometimes breaking the "rules" is more Christian than keeping them. For example, comforting a friend who is in pain on a Sunday morning might be more important than going to church. Is there an area in your life where the rules have become more important than being like Jesus? If so, what is one step you can take to get your priorities straight?

Checkup

___ I read pages 44–45.
___ I opened my prayer file and prayed the Show Me Prayer (pp. 8–9).
___ I bragged on someone (p. 11).
___ I walked around walls this week (p. 10).
___ I did unto others this week (p. 12).
___ I memorized a Bible verse this week.

Read Luke 14:1–14.

1 What did Jesus notice when the guests were taking their places at the table? How would you describe the attitude of the guests?

2 What are ways people today try to show their importance?

3 Why do you think the Pharisees had no answer to Jesus (verses 4 and 6)?

4 Shade in the pieces of pie below that indicate how proud you are compared to how humble you are.

Humble Pie

5 Jesus shows in this passage his willingness to heal people no matter the circumstances or timing. In what circumstances or places do you have a hard time being willing to serve? Explain. Could there be a solution to this? If so, what might it be?

6 Was there a time this past week when you had difficulty humbly putting others first? What do you think Jesus' advice would be to you?

Checkup

_____ I opened my prayer file and prayed the Show Me Prayer (pp. 8–9).
_____ I bragged on someone (p. 11).
_____ I walked around walls this week (p. 10).
_____ I did unto others this week (p. 12).
_____ I memorized a Bible verse this week.

Read John 1:1-18.

1 Verse 14 gives us the amazing news that the "Word became flesh" (NIV). That is, God became human—in the person of Jesus. Now let's try one of those confusing questions you find on the SAT tests.

God becoming human

is like

humans becoming _____.

2 God became man! This goes far beyond kneeling down. It was not only service, but sacrifice. What could you do that would take kneeling down a little further and would be sacrificing something important to you because of the love you have for someone else?

3 What is the greatest story—real or fictional—of "kneeling down" in service that you have heard or seen? Briefly summarize it and explain why you felt it was so great.

4 Christ came to earth in remarkable humility, but his own did not receive him (verse 11). What consequences might a typical person of importance inflict on those of lower status who rejected him or her?

5 Go back and look through the names in the pages of your prayer file (Action Step 1, pp. 8–9). Whose name sticks out to you that you could encourage and brag on today? What could you say and how could you go about doing it?

6 Take a moment for quiet reflection and ask God who or what group of people he would like you to serve in a simple and practical way for Action Step 4 (p. 12) this week and/or in the weeks to come.

Checkup

_____ I opened my prayer file and prayed the Show Me Prayer (pp. 8–9).
_____ I bragged on someone (p. 11).
_____ I walked around walls this week (p. 10).
_____ I did unto others this week (p. 12).
_____ I memorized a Bible verse this week.

Day 25

Read Matthew 20:20–28.

1 In what ways do parents today try to position their children ahead of others? According to this passage, what might Jesus say to them?

2 Come up with elements of a newspaper article about a story of service in your home, youth group, church, school, or community. (If you don't know of one, do some research or ask some questions—be a reporter.) Start with a headline.

3 What is the lead idea of your story or the hook that will keep the readers reading?

4 Where would you place the story in a newspaper and why? (For example, the front page, the business section, entertainment, and so on.)

5 Based on Jesus' words in verses 26–27, who might he name as some of the greatest in your youth group or church?

6 Jesus mentions the bitter cup he is about to drink from and does not create an illusion that service is easy. What is a situation where you served despite great difficulty? How did this make you feel? How did you grow?

Checkup

___ I opened my prayer file and prayed the Show Me Prayer (pp. 8–9).
___ I bragged on someone (p. 11).
___ I walked around walls this week (p. 10).
___ I did unto others this week (p. 12).
___ I memorized a Bible verse this week.

Day 26 Thursday date

Read Luke 9:28–48.

1 If you were Peter or James or John on that mountaintop, what would you be thinking and feeling? Why?

2 In what ways does our culture reflect Jesus' teaching in verse 48? In what ways does our culture work against his teaching?

3 In what ways can you welcome a "little child"?
_ Baby-sit
_ Help those who aren't able to help themselves
_ Become a professional diaper changer
_ Recognize the value in all people
_ Invest money in a toy store
_ Start a Children's Union
_ Do unto someone who is younger than you
_ Treat your younger brothers and sisters nicer
_ Get to know a kid in your church better
_ Other_____

4 What does Jesus mean when he says, "Whoever is the least among you is the greatest"?

5 Has opening a prayer file (see pp. 8–9) made a difference in your "kneeling down" to serve the world around you? If so, how?

6 Jesus walked around all kinds of walls to serve people no matter where they were, or who they were. If you haven't already completed your prayer walk this week for Action Step 2 (p. 10), what are your plans this time? If you've already done it, what was the experience like for you?

Checkup

_____ I opened my prayer file and prayed the Show Me Prayer (pp. 8–9).
_____ I bragged on someone (p. 11).
_____ I walked around walls this week (p. 10).
_____ I did unto others this week (p. 12).
_____ I memorized a Bible verse this week.

Day 27 friday date

Read Luke 22:24–30.

1 This passage begins with the disciples arguing once again about who was the greatest. Apparently this was an important issue for them. In what areas of your life is that question important to you?

2 When you think "leader," what five words come to mind? After reading Luke 22:24–30, what five words describe Jesus' idea of a leader?

My Words	Jesus' Words
1.	
2.	
3.	
4.	
5.	

3 When you eat at a restaurant, what is your typical attitude toward your server? Do Christ's words in verse 27 surprise you? Why or why not?

4 Who has remained true to you when you've gone through times of trial? What has that meant to you?

5 Is there someone you know who is going through a trial right now who you could stand by? If so, how could you stand by him or her? If not, how could you find someone to stand by that is having a tough time and needs some support?

6 Have your thoughts, feelings, or actions about kneeling down and serving changed after reading the Bible passages and answering the questions for this week? If so, how?

Checkup

___ I did Days 21–27.
___ I opened my prayer file and prayed the Show Me Prayer (pp. 8–9).
___ I bragged on someone (p. 11).
___ I walked around walls this week (p. 10).
___ I did unto others this week (p. 12).
___ I memorized a Bible verse this week.
___ I found the story behind the story (pp. 13–14).

51

Theme 5:
Speak Out

Sometimes your math class seems like a foreign language, doesn't it? "Solve the simultaneous equation for the coefficient of the secant in opposition to the hypotenuse." *Stop!* you want to cry. Use real words for a change.

Ever try to get tech support for your computer? "Connect the USB and make sure the SCSI chain is terminated, then go into the BIOS and . . . ." Thanks a lot.

Often, when we try to explain our faith to others, we sound as if we're speaking a foreign language. Salvation, redemption, conviction, repentance—we might as well be teaching calculus. Even simple ideas like being "saved" from our "sin" can go right over people's heads. They don't know those words like we do.

So we have to speak their language. But it's not just a matter of the words we use. Thanks to MTV and *Sesame Street*, people now think in *pictures* and *stories*. As you try to tell people what you believe, look for the word-pictures that tell the Jesus story.

This really isn't all that new. Jesus himself used parables to teach people about God's kingdom. What were parables? Stories that used word-pictures from everyday life. He avoided religious jargon and used the everyday life of his listeners to communicate profound truth.

Okay, now it's your turn. So far in this Adventure you've been praying, walking around, encouraging, and serving. Pretty easy stuff. But now it's time to speak out. How are you going to do that? By preaching theology? Of course not. Do what Jesus did: Use the stuff they're already talking about.

Start by listening for a few days. What are the people around you talking about? Their experiences. Sports. Other kids' experiences. Movies. TV. Music. All of this is your new vocabulary. As you seek to tell the story of Jesus, use the stories you hear people talking about. Look for examples of love, sacrifice, salvation (rescue), commitment, sin and its consequences, and renewal.

You don't have to tell the whole story every time. You want to develop an ongoing dialogue with people, so don't turn every experience into a passion play. "That detention you got is sort of like hell—a punishment for sin—and when Coach got you out of it, it was like he died for your sins." You might just want to say: "I wonder what Coach had to give to help you out."

Ask good questions. Jesus often used this tactic. You see, people know when you start preaching, and they put up their defenses. But questions draw them out, making them really think about something. For instance, there have been numerous songs lately that use religious language in describing romantic relationships. You could say, "Obviously these songwriters need to give their hearts to Jesus," but that's not your concern. Try asking: "When they say they need a 'savior,' what do they need to be saved from? Do you think a romance really meets those needs?"

Encouraging and serving people will win you the right to talk about your faith, but eventually you'll need to speak out. When you do, make sure you're using the words—and word-pictures—that people can hear.

FAQ: How do you "find the story behind the story?

Jason wasn't sure he knew how to use movies to talk about his faith, but he figured he'd give it a try. What was the worst that could happen? He and his friends would see an interesting movie or two. If he couldn't think of anything "Christian" to say, he'd just keep quiet.

So he planned a video night and invited a bunch of friends. A few people turned him down, but most were glad to have something to do on a Friday night besides standing around at the coffee shop. He made sure to invite the Angels—Ashley, Kim, and Lindsey—but only Ashley gave him a definite yes. Lindsey said maybe.

To prep, Jason watched TV shows that week and talked with his sister about them. Nikki was brutal, shooting down all lame ideas. After a rerun of *Friends*, he said, "Well, Jesus is our friend."

"Nice try," Nikki sneered.

After *Buffy*, Jason said, "Well, it makes me think about how Jesus slays the forces of evil in order to save us."

"Too easy," said his little sister. "I think you have to talk about the problem first before you jump to Jesus. I mean, it sounds like you're preaching."

What did she know? She's only twelve.

Jason picked up a couple of videos for $1—*Armageddon* and *The Truman Show*. He saw Armageddon when it came out, and he remembered liking it, but that was about it. He'd never seen *Truman* but he heard it was good. He decided to get two in case everyone hated one of them.

Friday night, there were already six people claiming the choice seats in Jason's living room when he opened the door to find Ashley there, with Lindsey right behind her.

"Are we late?" Lindsey cooed. "It's my fault."

"No, never," Jason stammered. "C-Come on in. Popcorn and pop are in there, and we've reserved you the best seat in the house—on the floor next to me."

The girls entered, giggling, just as Nikki was heading out. "Smooth, Romeo," she sneered.

The group voted to see *Armageddon* first. Some had seen it before, but it was pretty exciting with cool effects. Worth another view. During the movie, Jason tried to study it for ways he could talk about his faith. That wasn't easy with Lindsey sitting tantalizingly close to him.

After the movie, Jason said, "So this is a movie-and-discussion night, so let's discuss."

"Two thumbs up," said Dave Bristol. "It was so great when all that stuff was blowing up."

"I figured you'd like that," Jason smirked.

"It had some surprises," said Julie, who came with Jason's lockermate, Rob. "I expected them to succeed right away. It was kind of sad when they didn't."

"Yeah," Rob added, "and then Bruce Willis had to give himself up. That was powerful."

"Why?" asked Jason.

"Because you knew he was going to die to save everyone."

Lindsey piped up. "I thought there would be a miracle, so he wouldn't have to die."

"But that would ruin it," Jason replied. "He had to die. He was the sacrifice."

Lindsey wasn't getting it, but Julie and Rob were. Even Dave Bristol got it.

"That's right," said Ashley. "Salvation doesn't mean much unless it costs something. It's like Christianity. If Jesus didn't really die, he couldn't save us."

"But because he did," Jason added, "we can be free."

Rob was thinking seriously now. "I don't know anything about Jesus, but you're right about this movie. If Bruce Willis doesn't die, it's a happier movie, but it's dumb. That made it more real."

"But why do you think they called it *Armageddon*?" asked Dave.

The discussion went on that night, with Ashley, Jason, Lindsey and their non-Christian friends conversing at a level they'd never known before. They watched the second movie, too, and talked about meaning and purpose and humanity and God. No one actually became a Christian that night, but a few people edged closer to an understanding of what Jesus is all about. And they saw a couple of interesting movies.

S
P
E
A
K

O
U
T

Read Matthew 7:15–29.

1 What word-pictures did Jesus use in this passage that would have been familiar to his audience?

2 Pick one of the word-pictures you listed above and think of something similar that would be relevant to people today.

3 What aspects of popular culture could you use to find the story behind the story (see Action Step 5, pp. 13–14)?
_ Movies
_ TV shows
_ Monster truck rallies
_ Extreme sports
_ TV commercials
_ Best-selling books
_ Magazines
_ Music
_ Music videos
_ Video games
_ News stories
_ Personal stories
_ Sporting events
_ Other _____
_ Other _____
_ Other _____

4 Which of the above do you think would be the most powerful? Which are you the most familiar with? Which are you most comfortable with?

5 Describe your thoughts and plans for finding the story behind the story and completing Action Step 5 (pp. 13–14).

Checkup
_____ I read pages 52–53.
_____ I opened my prayer file and prayed the Show Me Prayer (pp. 8–9).
_____ I bragged on someone (p. 11).
_____ I walked around walls this week (p. 10).
_____ I did unto others this week (p. 12).
_____ I memorized a Bible verse this week.
_____ I found the story behind the story (pp. 13–14).

Read Matthew 6:1–8, 16–18.

1 Jesus paints vivid pictures of the hypocrites to show how not to give, pray, and fast. What pictures would you use to illustrate hypocrisy today?

2 What positive pictures of giving, prayer, and fasting would you use today?

3 Give a letter grade (A to F) to each of the following "Christian" activities.

___ Loudly praying in the cafeteria, asking God to smite the bacteria in the "mystery meat"

___ Sharing a "Bible verse of the day" with a few friends at your locker each morning

___ Telling everyone you're fasting when you're really just eating at "fast food" places

___ Telling a friend you'll pray for them to pass a tough test

___ Wearing a WWJD T-shirt

___ Carrying a boom box through town, blaring Carman hits

___ Meeting with classmates to pray at the flagpole before school

___ When you're invited to a party, responding, "I'll pray about it."

___ Asking friends to contribute to a hunger-relief project

4 There are many ways to "speak" to non-Christians. You can use your voice, your actions, your love, your life, and so on. In what way do you think you best speak to your world?

5 What is the most uncomfortable way for you to speak to your world?

6 This passage is part of Christ's Sermon on the Mount. If your pastor or youth leader were this direct, how would various hearers respond?

Checkup

___ I opened my prayer file and prayed the Show Me Prayer (pp. 8–9).

___ I bragged on someone (p. 11).

___ I walked around walls this week (p. 10).

___ I did unto others this week (p. 12).

___ I memorized a Bible verse this week.

___ I found the story behind the story (pp. 13–14).

Day 31 tuesday date

Read Luke 12:13-21.

1 In your own words, what is the point Jesus is trying to make in this parable? Do you think Jesus would have been as effective if he had just stated his point plainly? Explain.

2 What movie have you seen that you could use to talk about greed? How could you use that movie to illustrate the same points Jesus makes in this parable?

3 Are you comfortable talking with non-Christians about Jesus? Why or why not?

4 If Jesus had said, "Don't be greedy," do you think the man would have listened? How does a story explain the problem, entice a person to listen, and explore alternatives better than Ten-Commandment-style preaching? Explain.

5 What precautions and/or preparations can you take to make sure you are not preaching inappropriately, but instead speaking out to your friends about Jesus in a way they understand?

Checkup

_____I opened my prayer file and prayed the Show Me Prayer (pp. 8–9).
_____I bragged on someone (p. 11).
_____I walked around walls this week (p. 10).
_____I did unto others this week (p. 12).
_____I memorized a Bible verse this week.
_____I found the story behind the story (pp. 13–14).

Read Luke 12:22-34.

1 Jesus consistently addressed common, everyday problems. Looking back over this passage, what would Jesus say to your friends who worry?

2 What music have you heard that you could use to talk about the problem of worrying? What would you say?

3 What do you treasure? What does that show about where your heart is?

4 What or who in our society today uses powerful word-pictures to get a point across? Explain.

5 Think of a time in your life when you used a movie, song, or some other word-picture communication to explain a point you were trying to make. Why did you do that? How did your point come across?

6 Action Step 5 for this Adventure is to find the story behind the story (see pp. 13-14). If you haven't completed Action Step 5 yet, how do you plan to go about it? If you've finished, describe your experience.

Checkup

___I opened my prayer file and prayed the Show Me Prayer (pp. 8-9).
___I bragged on someone (p. 11).
___I walked around walls this week (p. 10).
___I did unto others this week (p. 12).
___I memorized a Bible verse this week.
___I found the story behind the story (pp. 13-14).

Day 33 thursday date

Read Matthew 25:31–46.

1 How could you use one of the following elements to tell a similar story?
- Baggy pants • *The X-Files* • Extreme sports • Nose rings
- The next *Star Wars* prequel • Guitar playing • Kosovo

2 Jesus, who attracted so many people, said he could be seen in the hungry, the sick, the prisoner, and so on. Name someone you believe sees Christ in those kinds of people today.

3 Each week of this Adventure you have been serving someone in a practical way for Action Step 4 (p. 12). What common element of your culture could you use to tell your experience of this service to one of your friends?

4 Some of the most powerful word-pictures we can use to show Jesus to our friends are very personal stories of our own lives. How could you go about the telling of your story to a friend without being preachy?

5 What would it take for you to tell that story? How would you go about doing that?

6 For practice, write your story and store it in your prayer file (see Action Step 1, pp. 8–9).

Checkup

_____ I opened my prayer file and prayed the Show Me Prayer (pp. 8–9).
_____ I bragged on someone (p. 11).
_____ I walked around walls this week (p. 10).
_____ I did unto others this week (p. 12).
_____ I memorized a Bible verse this week.
_____ I found the story behind the story (pp. 13–14).

Day 34 friday date

Read Luke 18:1–8.

1 What lesson did Jesus teach the disciples with this story?

2 As a contemporary follower of Christ, are you ever tempted to stop praying and give up? What does this story say to you?

3 Does this story mean we have to be annoying in order to get results? Why or why not?

4 What is the most powerful story of this Adventure for you? Explain.

5 What movie could you use to explain to your friends something meaningful about your Adventure experience? Why did you choose this movie?

6 If you haven't yet found the story behind the story and completed Action Step 5 (pp. 13–14), consider inviting your friends over to see the movie you mentioned in question 5, and let the discussion bring out your Adventure experience. How could you go about doing this?

Checkup

_____ I did Days 28-34.
_____ I opened my prayer file and prayed the Show Me Prayer (pp. 8–9).
_____ I bragged on someone (p. 11).
_____ I walked around walls this week (p. 10).
_____ I did unto others this week (p. 12).
_____ I memorized a Bible verse this week.
_____ I found the story behind the story (pp. 13–14).

5 9

Theme 6: Look Ahead

What's this world coming to?

You hear people asking that more and more, as senseless violence rocks our globe. Up until a decade ago, people worried about one of the major nations starting a nuclear war. That seems less likely now, but we still fret about terrorists. And nowadays any kid can find directions for making a pipe bomb on the Internet.

What are you going to be if you grow up?

Aren't you tired of people asking you that? As if being grown up is all that. And who knows what kind of world will be there in a couple of years anyway. Computers are driving us faster and faster. Technology is building the new century so rapidly, it's hard to keep up. The only thing we do know is that we don't know anything about the future at all.

So what's the point?

What's driving you, and the people around you? What kind of life do you want to create for yourself in five years or in a decade or even two? Do you have a 2020 vision? Make a lot of money? Maybe. Have a family? What if your marriage doesn't work out? Get famous? Even a bigger maybe. Why not just spend your life snowboarding all weekend, skating through life, and surfing the Net?

You're probably not really this depressed. I know that. But when you think about the future, what do you find besides the question marks? Your grandparents, maybe even your parents, could stand where you are and map out a future for themselves. But your world is different than the one they saw. There is no certainty and not too much safety either.

But you do have something to hang on to. You may not know what the future holds, but you know who holds the future. You are part of a plan that stretches through all time. You are a part of God's plan.

Jesus talked about God's kingdom all the time. Most of his parables described it. He spoke of it as a crisp reality that you could reach out and touch, but it also stood at the end of the world as we know it. It's where we are, and it's where we're headed. God's kingdom exists wherever God is King. It's in your heart, in your relationships, in your church, and in your future.

God's kingdom is full of surprises—happy surprises for those of us who aren't too sure of ourselves. The last come in first, the humble are exalted, the meek rewarded. If you sell all you have and invest in God's kingdom, you get a huge payoff. But if you rebel, running off and wasting your resources, come on back anyhow—you'll find forgiveness in the Father's outspread arms. Surprise!

In a world that doesn't know its way, we can put up signposts. THIS WAY TO FIND MEANING. For those who wonder what this world is coming to, we can say, "I know." And to people who wonder where *they're* going when they grow up, if they grow up, we can say, "There is a plan." If you let God be the King of your life, you'll find a meaning, a purpose, and a plan—no matter what you do or where you go. There *is* a point to this crazy thing called life.

Ashley had a short drama club meeting after school, short enough to be pretty useless, long enough to make her miss the three o'clock bus. It was a nice day, though. She sat on the front steps of the school waiting for the late bus, half-reading her chemistry textbook.

She was startled when a guy came tearing out of the building, halfway to the street, looked up and saw no buses there, then stopped short. He checked his watch and looked around.

"They're gone," she said. The guy looked familiar. "You're Jason's friend, aren't you?" Ashley asked. "From the video night?"

"Right," he smiled. "I'm Rob, and you're, uh, Ashley." She nodded, and he moved closer, angling a foot on the steps. "That was fun, the videos."

"Yeah," Ashley responded, looking up from her book.

"Fun to talk about them. It's like they mean something."

Lull. There was a moment when both paused to reload the conversation. Ashley realized that she should probably say something about her faith, but she couldn't think of anything. Rob obviously wanted to talk, but she was just offering single syllables.

"You're a senior, right?" she asked him.

"Yep."

"Me too. What are you doing next year?"

"Dunno yet," Rob said, kicking the cement. "Community college, maybe. I might just work."

"What field are you interested in?" Ashley suddenly worried she sounded like a parent.

Still looking down, he answered, "No idea. How 'bout you?"

"I love drama. And writing. I love a lot of things really. But I really want to help people."

"Yeah." He looked up at her. "That sounds good. I guess I don't really know what I want."

Ashley saw the aimlessness in Rob, like so many of her classmates. What could she say? She was so bad at this. How could she ever help people if she never knew the right thing to say?

"Maybe . . . ," she started, and stopped, reforming her thoughts. "Maybe it's not that important, what you want. I mean, last fall I really wanted to get the lead role in *Our Town*. I studied and prepared and had a great audition, and I didn't get it. I don't know why. But after that something happened to me. *Started* happening to me. I started spending more time with God, praying and reading the Bible, you know? And I began to realize that what I wanted wasn't so great. What did God want? That was the question. He had something in mind for me, something really good, if I would just let him do it."

Rob was studying her face as she talked. She suddenly felt self-conscious. "I'm sorry," she stammered. "That probably sounds weird to you."

"No," he said quickly. "No, it's good. I don't have that. I don't know what God wants for me. I guess I don't think about God very much."

"Well . . . ," Ashley started, and stopped again.

Reading her mind, Rob added, "Yeah, maybe I should," but then looked very uncomfortable. "Hey, I just realized I left something in my locker. I gotta go back in. It's been nice talking to you."

"Yes," Ashley answered, worrying that she'd said something wrong. "Rob!" she called after him. "You know what I think? I think God has great plans for you. I don't know what they are, but it'll be exciting to see. That's what I think."

He stood a moment, transfixed, as if standing on the edge of a cliff. "Thanks," he said finally, and ran inside.

Ashley picked up her chemistry text and continued reading about the transformation of molecules.

LOOK AHEAD

Read Matthew 4:23—5:12.

1 If you were telling a friend about the great benefits of following Christ, what specific examples would you give?

2 What are Jesus' main activities in verses 23–25, and how did they improve the lives of those around him?

3 What does Jesus have to say to kids in your school or neighborhood who feel like outcasts, who are mocked and made fun of?

4 What does Jesus have to say to the kids in your school who are victims of rape, physical abuse, or any other crime or abuse?

5 What does Jesus have to say to kids who show kindness to the outcast and abused, who try to bring people together in peace, and who strive to show God's love to their world?

6 Open your prayer file and reread this passage, listening for Jesus' word to you—whether of comfort or challenge. Write down what you feel Jesus is telling you.

Checkup

____ I read pages 60–61.
____ I opened my prayer file and prayed the Show Me Prayer (pp. 8–9).
____ I bragged on someone (p. 11).
____ I walked around walls this week (p. 10).
____ I did unto others this week (p. 12).
____ I memorized a Bible verse this week.
____ I found the story behind the story (pp. 13–14).

Day 37 monday date

Read Luke 4:16–21.

1 Which of the five ministries of Christ in verses 18–19 is particularly appealing to you? Why?

2 What did Jesus mean when he said, "This Scripture has come true today before your very eyes"?

3 What do these verses have to say to your non-Christian friends?

4 There are many people in your school and community who need to "look ahead" to something. What friends do you know of who are uncertain, aimless, or worried about the future? Could you brag on some of these friends this week for Action Step 3 (p. 11)? (See if you can come up with at least five friends, and try to brag on one each day for the rest of the week.)

Today:
Tuesday:
Wednesday:
Thursday:
Friday:

5 What could you do or say to your friends to encourage them to "look ahead"?

6 Action Step 2 for this Adventure is to walk around walls and do a prayer walk each week (p. 10). What plans or steps do you need to take to make sure you complete this Action Step for the next two weeks? Who could you invite along that you haven't already?

Checkup
____I opened my prayer file and prayed the Show Me Prayer (pp. 8–9).
____I bragged on someone (p. 11).
____I walked around walls this week (p. 10).
____I did unto others this week (p. 12).
____I memorized a Bible verse this week.
____I found the story behind the story (pp. 13–14).

L O O K   A H E A D

Read Matthew 12:46–50.

1 Who belongs to the family of Jesus? Who are his brothers and sisters?
_ You
_ The kids in your youth group
_ The people at church
_ The people at other churches
_ Christians in other countries
_ Other Christians at school
_ Non-Christians
_ Soon-to-be Christians
_ Christians you don't like
_ Someone who does God's will
_ Other

2 Although family relationships are clearly important in the Bible, how do Jesus' words in this passage encourage us to think about our fellow believers?

3 Do you think non-Christians perceive that Christians have loving, "new family" relationships? What kinds of behavior among Christians might negatively impact nonbelievers' views of the church?

4 Action Step 4 for this Adventure is to do unto others by serving them in a simple and practical way (see p. 12). What could you do for someone this week to help him or her to look ahead and see a bright future? How would you go about doing that?

5 Who in your church or youth group is becoming like family to you?

6 For your church or youth group to really become like family to you, what is one step you could take today?

Checkup
___ I opened my prayer file and prayed the Show Me Prayer (pp. 8–9).
___ I bragged on someone (p. 11).
___ I walked around walls this week (p. 10).
___ I did unto others this week (p. 12).
___ I memorized a Bible verse this week.
___ I found the story behind the story (pp. 13–14).

Day 39

wednesdaydate

Read John 7:37–39.

1 According to Jesus, who is entitled to "living water"? What does the image of water communicate to you about the Spirit?

2 What are some of the benefits you experience because the Holy Spirit lives in you?

3 When recently were you aware of the Holy Spirit's work in your life? Describe the experience.

4 Reflecting on your past experiences, how has the presence of the Spirit changed your life or satisfied your spiritual thirst?

5 Often we say, "I can't imagine life without . . ." If you were telling someone why you can't picture life without the Spirit, what would you say?

6 How could you communicate Jesus' offer to your friends? How would you go about doing that? Is this something you want to do?

Checkup

_____ I opened my prayer file and prayed the Show Me Prayer (pp. 8–9).
_____ I bragged on someone (p. 11).
_____ I walked around walls this week (p. 10).
_____ I did unto others this week (p. 12).
_____ I memorized a Bible verse this week.
_____ I found the story behind the story (pp. 13–14).

LOOK AHEAD

Read John 6:35–40.

1 What kind of future is Jesus promising his disciples?
(Check all that apply.)
  _ The respect of all your friends
  _ Resurrection
  _ Peace of mind
  _ A really cool car
  _ Eternal life
  _ The finest community college education money can buy
  _ The will of God
  _ Success in ministry
  _ Revenge on people who treated them badly
  _ A chance to star in the next Shania Twain video
  _ Other_____

2 Which of the promises in this passage apply primarily to the future?
Which apply today?

_____

3 How do you feel when you look ahead? What do you look ahead to? How
do your non-Christian friends feel about their future? What do they look
ahead to?

4 Think of a recent movie that offers a look ahead and an idea of the
future. How could you use this movie to find the story behind the story
with your friends (see Action Step 5, pp. 13–14)?

5 Christ has promised to raise up believers at the last day. How does that
promise influence the way you live?

6 Who is someone who seems uncertain of his or her future or seems lost
that you wish could live in that hope? Take a moment to pray for that
person and add him or her to your prayer file.

Checkup
  _____ I opened my prayer file and prayed the Show Me Prayer (pp. 8–9).
  _____ I bragged on someone (p. 11).
  _____ I walked around walls this week (p. 10).
  _____ I did unto others this week (p. 12).
  _____ I memorized a Bible verse this week.
  _____ I found the story behind the story (pp. 13–14).

Day 41

Read John 14:1–7.

1 Jesus himself is going ahead to prepare a place for his followers. How does that make you feel?

2 In what ways do you see heaven as infinitely better than this present life?

3 In this passage Jesus says, "Trust in me." How do you show trust?
_ Do what he says
_ Walk barefoot over hot coals
_ Instead of studying, pray!
_ Let Jesus revise your view of success
_ Honor your parents
_ Read the Bible for guidance
_ Call Sunday your day of rest and refuse to get out of bed
_ Hang out with other Christians
_ Refuse to hang out with non-Christians
_ Other _____

4 Jesus also says, "Don't be troubled." What are you troubled or scared about? Do Jesus' words and the future you have to look ahead to help you not be troubled? Why or why not?

5 When have you experienced a glimpse of heaven on earth?

6 What is the biggest idea, thought, or feeling you would like to share with your friends from this last week of the Adventure? Who would you especially like to share with? How could you go about doing that?

7 If you look ahead to the end of this Adventure, what do you see? How do you think you will look back on this experience? Will any of the action steps or ideas of this Adventure stay with you or make a difference in your future? Explain.

Checkup
_____ I did Days 35–41.
_____ I opened my prayer file and prayed the Show Me Prayer (pp. 8–9).
_____ I bragged on someone (p. 11).
_____ I walked around walls this week (p. 10).
_____ I did unto others this week (p. 12).
_____ I memorized a Bible verse this week.
_____ I found the story behind the story (pp. 13–14).

Theme 7:
Follow Through

"Hey, I'll call you sometime; we'll do something."

Uh-huh. What are the chances of that ever happening? Depends on the person. But you've probably had your fill of unkept promises, abandoned plans, and people who just don't follow through.

A week before the school play opens Joe drops out. "It's no fun anymore," he says, ignoring the fact that the rest of the cast has to scramble to fill in his scenes.

Or you snag some tickets to see that great ska band you love, but that afternoon your best friend Rachel decides not to go. No reason. She just doesn't feel like it. *But who's going to pay for this $50 ticket?* And so you're frantically making phone calls all afternoon because your former best friend Rachel didn't follow through.

It's refreshing when you meet someone who keeps promises, who sticks to a commitment, who knows where they're going and keeps on going, wherever the winds may blow.

Jesus was like that. He had a mission, and it wasn't an easy one. He was headed to the cross, and he wouldn't let anything stand in his way. "No, not you," said his good buddy Pete. "You're not going to die in Jerusalem." But Jesus saw that comment as the temptation it was. "Get behind me, Satan!" he barked. Make no mistake—Jesus was following through on his mission.

What's your mission? Maybe you're still figuring that out, and that's fine. But it will have something to do with living for God, advancing his kingdom, sharing Jesus with others, letting God get more glory. God has given you certain abilities that he will use for his purposes. Are you going to follow through and complete the mission he gives you?

In a world of broken promises, your sense of commitment will stand out. You may not be Miss Popularity, but people will be strangely attracted to your dedication. They will learn that you're reliable. They'll see that you're headed somewhere, not drifting aimlessly like so many others.

How can you get on that track? How can you make it happen? Here are some pointers:

Be aware of your unique calling. You may not have the same exact mission as the other Christians in your youth group. You have different gifts. You're all serving God, but in different ways. Maybe you're an encourager instead of a preacher; great! But then get serious about encouraging. Once Peter asked about the Lord's plans for John. "What is that to you?" Jesus answered. "You follow me!"

Be ready to suffer. The way of Jesus isn't cushy. Some have faced torture and death for Christ's sake. That probably won't happen to you. But you may face misunderstanding, rejection, ridicule. James and John wanted to sit next to Jesus in his kingdom, taking seats of honor. Jesus said, "Sure, if you're ready to drink the cup of suffering."

Be willing to fail. It's risky business when you're on a mission from God. You have to try some new things, things you may not be good at. God is always testing your faith, asking you to rely on him for strength. Following Christ isn't a safe game of badminton in the back yard; it's the X-Games.

Be open to surprises. Guaranteed: God will surprise you. Don't get so locked into your own sense of mission that you stop listening for daily instructions. He may shift your mission suddenly. He may snatch victory out of sure defeat. He will use you in ways you've never imagined. Bet on it.

FAQ: Don't you realize how hard it is to "share Jesus with a friend"?

The Adventure was over. No more bragging on a different person every day. No more weekly acts of service. Jason tried to keep his "prayer file" going, but he missed a few days. Ashley was planning another prayer walk. Sometimes the Adventure plants seeds that keep growing.

The school was basking in those lazy days of May, when the weather outside makes every indoor moment feel wasted. But important things were happening on two opposite sides of the school. Jason was in the gym shooting hoops with his friend Rob. Ashley was at a table in the library, sitting across from a troubled girl she didn't know.

The girl was fidgeting in her chair, and that kept Ashley from concentrating on the Edgar Allan Poe story she was reading. Ashley was about to complain, but when she looked up, she noticed the girl doodling furiously in a notebook. The page was a sea of images—faces, lightning bolts, guitars, guns—all surrounding a large heart that was broken in two. In that moment, something touched Ashley's heart. Her complaint turned to compassion.

"Hard to work on a day like today," she said.

"Mmmmm," the girl answered, still intent on her doodling.

"My name's Ashley."

The girl looked up suddenly with her eyes, her face an open window. "Oh, I'm Trish."

Jason couldn't make a basket to save his life. Rob was sinking three-pointers right and left. After several futile shots, Jason just started fetching the ball and tossing it back to Rob.

"You've got the touch," he said.

Rob smiled bleakly. Nothing but net. "At least there's *something* I can do."

"Listen, Rob," Jason began. He had been wanting to say something for weeks, but had chickened out. Here was his opportunity. "We've got kind of a game night at my church this Friday. Some volleyball first and then pizza. You want to come?"

"I don't like church."

So that was that. Jason tried, and his effort fell short. Rob wasn't interested in church. But there was a voice inside Jason saying, *Dig deeper.* He fired a pass at his friend and asked, "Why?"

"Bunch of hypocrites." Rob made a deke move and launched a shot that circled the rim.

Dribbling around his friend, Jason asked, "Am I a hypocrite?"

"Oh, no. I didn't mean you."

Then silence. Just the basketball bouncing steadily. Rob had something to say.

"My dad. He went to church. Before he walked out."

"Oh." Bounce. Bounce. "Well, the truth is—" Jason said as he drove in for a lay-up and finally scored, "—I *am* a hypocrite. We all are. We know what's right and we don't do it."

"Well, no. I don't mean—"

"I'm serious, Rob. We don't go to church to show how holy we are. We go because we need God's forgiveness." Jason fired a pass. "Friday night is just for fun, but it's for sinners only."

"I wish I could draw like you," Ashley told Trish. "That's really great."

"I'm just doodling."

"Yeah, but it makes me feel something. That's what art needs to do. That's really vivid."

Trish wasn't sure whether she should trust this girl. She'd been mocked so many times. But there was some sort of peace in Ashley's voice. "There are so many things inside me," she said. "Things that hurt sometimes, and I want to get it all out on paper and I don't always have the words, so I draw. And it's like whatever is in me just comes out there. You know what I mean?"

"I think so," Ashley responded. "Do you have other drawings?"

No one became a Christian in that school on that day. Not yet. But two kids began to hear Jesus knocking at the door. And that happened because two other kids heard Jesus' voice and followed his directions. There are a million reasons not to share the love or truth of Jesus with others, but Ashley and Jason rose above those restraints and let Jesus have his way.

F O L L O W   T H R O U G H

Read Mark 11:1–19.

1 Write your own four line poem praising God like the one the crowd was shouting at Jesus (verses 9–10).

   1.

   2.

   3.

   4.

2 Jesus was fulfilling his mission and following through on God's will. Do you feel that God has a mission for you? If so, what might it be?

3 It's one thing knowing God's will and another thing following through. How hard or easy do you find it to follow through on what you know God wants you to do? Explain.

4 What could make it easier for you to follow through? What makes it harder?

5 How hard or easy has it been for you to follow through with this Adventure? Why?

Checkup

I read pages 68–69.

I opened my prayer file and prayed the Show Me Prayer (pp. 8–9).

I bragged on someone (p. 11).

I walked around walls this week (p. 10).

I did unto others this week (p. 12).

I memorized a Bible verse this week.

I found the story behind the story (pp. 13–14).

Day 44

monday date

Read Luke 20:9–19, 45–47.

1 Jesus has the courage to speak against the teachers of the Law even though it causes them to look for a way to arrest him. Have you ever shown courage in a situation even when you knew there would be some suffering involved? If so, when?

2 What are situations where you or someone you know is afraid of a negative response to being identified with Christ?

3 How does Jesus' example in this passage encourage you to respond when faced with rejection as a result of your faith?

4 When have you had a mission set out before you that you followed through with?

5 Is there an action step for this Adventure that you have yet to follow through on? If so, which one and how could you take care of that before the Adventure is over?

6 This week make it a point to notice every time someone follows through for you and let him or her know that you appreciate it.

Checkup

____ I opened my prayer file and prayed the Show Me Prayer (pp. 8–9).
____ I bragged on someone (p. 11).
____ I walked around walls this week (p. 10).
____ I did unto others this week (p. 12).
____ I memorized a Bible verse this week.
____ I found the story behind the story (pp. 13–14).

FOLLOW THROUGH

Day 45 tuesday date_____

Read John 15:18–25.

1 Does it surprise you when people today show hostility toward Christ? Why or why not?

2 Have you ever felt persecuted or hated for being a Christian or standing up for your Christian beliefs? If so, when?

3 On a scale of 1 to 47 how often do you feel like you do not belong to this world because of your faith?

1 ————————————————————————— 47

4 How do you feel about following through with your faith and beliefs even in the face of persecution or being seen as an outsider?

5 From this passage, it's clear that Jesus knew his arrest and crucifixion were just hours away. How does his courage in completing his assigned mission speak to you?

6 In what area of this Adventure have you felt you followed through the best? Why?

Checkup

_____ I opened my prayer file and prayed the Show Me Prayer (pp. 8–9).
_____ I bragged on someone (p. 11).
_____ I walked around walls this week (p. 10).
_____ I did unto others this week (p. 12).
_____ I memorized a Bible verse this week.
_____ I found the story behind the story (pp. 13–14).

Day 46

Read Luke 22:39–46.

1 Jesus knew he was about to be arrested and put to death. What are some words or phrases that describe the intensity of his prayer in this passage?

2 This passage makes it clear that prayer is important during trying times. Name some ways prayer could be helpful to you in a difficult situation.

3 On a scale of 1–97, how would you rate yourself in following Jesus' example of prayer and submission to God's will even in difficult circumstances? What does your answer reveal to you?

1 ———————————————————— 97

4 On a scale of 1 to 97 how much have you sacrificed to follow through with your faith? On the same scale, how much are you *willing* to sacrifice to follow through with your faith?

sacrificed
1 ———————————————————— 97
willing to sacrifice

5 In what area of this Adventure did you feel the most temptation to blow it off? How did you respond to that temptation?

6 The thief in this story is proof that even if you failed to follow through or do good in the past, God will bless you for the action you take *now*. On the left write down three things you failed to do in the past, and then cross them out. You are making a fresh start. Now, on the right write three things you will (with God's help) follow through on.

Failures   Follow Throughs
1.
2.
3.

Checkup

___ I opened my prayer file and prayed the Show Me Prayer (pp. 8–9).
___ I bragged on someone (p. 11).
___ I walked around walls this week (p. 10).
___ I did unto others this week (p. 12).
___ I memorized a Bible verse this week.
___ I found the story behind the story (pp. 13–14).

F O L L O W   T H R O U G H

Read Matthew 27:11–31.

1 Why was Jesus led away to be crucified?

2 In spite of flogging and beating Jesus continues to follow through with his mission. Who is someone you know about who has gone to great lengths and pain to follow through on his or her plans or mission? Summarize their story here.

3 What is one area in your life where you feel called to put aside personal comfort in order to obey God?

4 What in your life would you be the most willing to suffer and go through pain for?

5 When during this Adventure did you follow through even though it took some extra effort or suffering? Explain.

6 Jesus went through the ultimate agony and pain yet still submitted to God's will and followed through on his mission. Take some time to pray in your prayer file about your thankfulness and feelings about Jesus' sacrifice for you.

Checkup

I opened my prayer file and prayed the Show Me Prayer (pp. 8–9).
I bragged on someone (p. 11).
I walked around walls this week (p. 10).
I did unto others this week (p. 12).
I memorized a Bible verse this week.
I found the story behind the story (pp. 13–14).

Day 48

friday date _____

Read Mark 15:21–41.

1 Crucifixion was a particularly gruesome death. Which details strike you about the way the Son of God died?

2 What emotions and thoughts are stirred as you think about this passage?

3 What percentage did you follow through on the action steps?

Opening a prayer file	___ %
Walking around walls	___ %
Bragging on someone	___ %
Doing unto others	___ %
Finding the story behind the story	___ %

4 Which action steps were the easiest for you to follow through with?
  _ The daily ones
  _ The weekly one
  _ The ones you only had to do once
  _ All of them, they were easy
  _ None of them, they were all hard
  _ What's an action step?

What does this response tell you?

5 Has following through on something ever been so difficult that you felt God had forsaken you? If so, explain.

6 Congratulations! You're almost through the Adventure and you should be really proud of all that you've accomplished. If you feel you didn't do everything, don't feel guilty. You can always go back and do things later. And of course you could always repeat this Adventure to solidify all the great things you learned the first time around.

Checkup

____ I did Days 42–48.
____ I opened my prayer file and prayed the Show Me Prayer (pp. 8–9).
____ I bragged on someone (p. 11).
____ I walked around walls this week (p. 10).
____ I did unto others this week (p. 12).
____ I memorized a Bible verse this week.
____ I found the story behind the story (pp. 13–14).

FOLLOW THROUGH

7 ◄ 5

Theme 8:
Rise Above

Amazing what movies are doing these days with special effects. In some fight scenes, the people seem to jump impossibly high before delivering their kicks. They run up the walls to gain an advantage. It looks like they're breaking the laws of gravity, the laws of time and motion, as they leap high over their opponents to win the struggle.

Of course they do it with wires. Blue screens, camera tricks, and editing techniques conspire to make it look as if the impossible is actually happening. On the screen, it's just an illusion. It's a shame we can't rise above our foes like that in real life.

Or maybe we can.

Now before you start taking kickboxing lessons, let's think about the importance of *spiritual* power in our world. When Jesus walked the earth, he displayed this power, but not in a violent way. He healed people. He cast out the demons that were tormenting people. Once he even calmed a storm. When people heard him teach, they were amazed, because he taught with authority. He knew what he was talking about, and that gave him a kind of power, too. People wanted to touch his power, to use his power, to buy his power—and his enemies envied it.

They finally managed to kill him, thinking that would put an end to their problem. But Jesus' power was even stronger than death. He burst forth from the grave to cook breakfast for his disciples in Galilee.

Talk about breaking the rules! You want "special effects"? Jesus didn't just break the law of gravity; he broke the law of *the grave*. The rule is: You die and you stay dead. What goes down won't come up. But Jesus smashed that assumption to hell (literally). He changed everything.

Over breakfast, and for a few weeks afterward, Jesus taught his friends about the Holy Spirit who would come to live inside them—the Spirit of power. The awesome secret is that the same Spirit lives in you and me, in *all* of Jesus' friends. That's the Spirit that raised Jesus from the dead, and he's crashing at your place.

Which means you have spiritual power, if you choose to use it. Does that mean you can go around healing people? Maybe. Give it a try if you want to. But keep in mind that the most important healing is spiritual. People are blind to God's goodness, jailed by modern demons of lust and greed, deeply wounded by past experiences. You *do* have power to heal those problems, by bringing Jesus into their lives. In this world of human wreckage, you can use Christ's power to start putting the pieces back together.

Are you ready to break the rules? Are you ready to challenge the assumptions of the people around you? Are you ready to rise above the forces of pride and prejudice, cynicism and sin? Rise in the power of the resurrection and let God's Spirit lead you as you lead others to the light of Christ.

Read John 19:38–42.

1 This was the darkest of moments for Jesus' followers. Why do you think Joseph and Nicodemus chose at this time to openly identify themselves with Christ?

2 Has this Adventure helped you recognize the times when you might hesitate to speak out for Jesus? If so, how?

3 During the past seven weeks, in what ways have you been more open about your faith?

4 If you had the power to rise above anything in your life, what would it be?

5 Pray for God's power in that aspect of your life now. Is there someone who could support you in that effort? What plan of action will you make?

6 Name someone who needs to know that Christ has broken the power of darkness in your life so you can live in the light.

Checkup

_____ I read page 76.
_____ I opened my prayer file and prayed the Show Me Prayer (pp. 8–9).
_____ I bragged on someone (p. 11).
_____ I walked around walls this week (p. 10).
_____ I did unto others this week (p. 12).
_____ I memorized a Bible verse this week.
_____ I found the story behind the story (pp. 13–14).

Day 50
sunday date _____

Read Acts 26:1–18.

1 What task does Jesus assign Paul in verses 16–18? Is there a specific situation in your life where you sense Christ calling you to be "a witness of what you have seen" (NIV) of him?

2 In 23 words or less, describe how the resurrection of Jesus affects your daily life?

3 Has this Adventure helped you to rise above? If so, how?

4 How have the action steps been for you? Are there any action steps you would like to continue after this Adventure is over? Or is there one you would like to pursue a little deeper?

5 How have the eight themes of this Adventure been for you? Do you have a favorite? What do you want to remember about it?

6 Are there any themes from this Adventure that you would like to learn more about or dig deeper into? If so, which ones? How do you plan to do that? You might talk to your youth leader or pastor for ideas.

Checkup
_____ I did Days 1–50.
_____ I opened a prayer file.
_____ I walked around walls.
_____ I bragged on someone.
_____ I did unto others.
_____ I found the story behind the story.
_____ I memorized Bible verses that remind me of who Jesus really is and how I can use my life to share him with my friends.

Last Words

1 Take a look back on page 5 of this journal where you recorded your goal for this 50-Day Spiritual Adventure and your action plan. How well did you achieve your goal? Did you follow your action plan?

2 If you fell short of your goal, don't feel bad or guilty about it, there is still time. What can you do in the coming weeks to acheive this goal? How would you like to revise your goal or action plan?

3 As you finish up this Adventure don't forget about your prayer file. Make sure you go through it at least one last time. Look at your growth during the last 50 days. Look for things you want to remember to do or follow up on.

Final Checkup
_ I did Days 1–50.
_ I opened a prayer file.
_ I walked around walls.
_ I bragged on someone.
_ I did unto others.
_ I found the story behind the story.
_ I memorized Bible verses that remind me of who Jesus really is and how I can use my life to share him with my friends.

Tell us your story
We've been praying that this Adventure would make a difference in your life. And we would love to hear your story. As you're finishing up this Adventure, we're already hard at work on a new one. But the Adventure is for you. So send us your story. We'd love to hear from you. Or send an e-mail with your comments to: T50DSA@aol.com

Mainstay Church Resources
Editorial Department
PO Box 30
Wheaton, IL 60189

Item	Title	Retail	Qty	Total

The Jesus 50-Day Spiritual Adventure

Item	Title	Retail	Qty	Total
0020	The Jesus Student Journal	7.00	____	____
7870	The Jesus Student Scripture Pack	2.00	____	____

The Real Deal 50-Day Spiritual Adventure

2920	The Real Deal Student Journal	7.00	____	____
7846	The Real Deal Scripture Pack	2.00	____	____

Power Up 50-Day Spiritual Adventure

2820	Power Up Student Journal	6.00	____	____
7818	Tapped-Out Christian's Little Energy Pack	1.00	____	____

In the House 50-Day Spiritual Adventure

2720	In the House Student Journal	6.00	____	____
7796	Make It Happen Scripture Pack	1.00	____	____

I'm So Confused 50-Day Spiritual Adventure

2620	I'm So Confused Student Journal	6.00	____	____
7772	Believe It or Not Scripture Pack	1.00	____	____

SUBTOTAL _____

Add 10% for UPS shipping/handling ($4.00 minimum) _____

Add the appropriate sales tax in the following _____
states and Canada: Alabama, Arizona, California,
Connecticut, Georgia, Idaho, Illinois, Iowa, Kansas,
Louisiana, Maine, North Carolina, North Dakota,
South Dakota, Washington, Virginia, West Virginia.

TOTAL AMOUNT ENCLOSED _____

Ship my order to:

Name _____

Street Address* _____

City _____

State/Prov _____ Zip/Code _____ Phone ( ) _____

*Note: UPS will not deliver to a P.O. box.

Mail this form with your check made payable to:
Mainstay Church Resources, Box 30, Wheaton, IL 60189-0030
In Canada: The Chapel Ministries, Box 2000, Waterdown, ON L0R 2H0

For U.S. VISA, MasterCard, and Discover card orders, **call 1-800-224-2735.**
In Canada, **call 1-800-461-4114.**

M080SJ